Everyday Apologetics offers ma[...] topics, providing clear guidan[...] [...] faith [...] concise handbook on key faith questions can help embolden believers in their witness for Christ.

> **Paul Copan**, Pledger Family Chair of Philosophy and
> Ethics, Palm Beach Atlantic University (Florida);
> author of *Is God a Moral Monster?*

Have some questions as a Christian? Encountering objections online? Having difficulty answering your kids' questions about God and Jesus? *Everyday Apologetics* will help you investigate and respond to common objections to Christianity, so you can grow in your personal confidence and share the gospel with your friends and neighbors. Paul Chamberlain and Chris Price have assembled a winsome and practical collection of stories, illustrations, and information that will help you remove the mystery of "apologetics" and interact effectively with the world around you.

> **J. Warner Wallace**, *Dateline*-featured cold-case detective;
> author of *Cold-Case Christianity*; speaker and senior fellow
> at the Colson Center for Christian Worldview; adjunct
> professor of apologetics at Talbot School of Theology
> (Biola University) and Southern Evangelical Seminary

Everyday Apologetics is a great contribution to defending the Christian faith in today's culture. It has quite an array of contributors and addresses many of the critical issues in apologetics today while still being accessible to the non-scholar. It is a very helpful addition to the tools available to those interested in answering objections to Christian faith.

> **Scott B. Rae**, dean of faculty and professor of Christian
> ethics, Talbot School of Theology (Biola University)

This book is engaging—it is timely, witty, even funny. More importantly, it deals with today's thorniest problems without being academic or boring. Religious doubt, horrible examples of pain and suffering, scientific challenges to faith, and Christian exclusivity are all addressed. Moreover, a case for Christianity is also built, including numerous examples of practical application throughout the entire volume. Check it out. Highly recommended.

Gary R. Habermas, distinguished research professor and chair of the department of philosophy, Liberty University

everyday apologetics

everyday apologetics

answering common objections to the christian faith

PAUL CHAMBERLAIN
CHRIS PRICE · EDITORS

JASON BALLARD · **MARK CLARK**
KIRK DURSTON · **MICHAEL HORNER**
JON MORRISON · **BARTON PRIEBE**
ANDY STEIGER · AUTHORS

---

foreword by sean mcdowell

LEXHAM PRESS

Everyday Apologetics: Answering Common Objections to the Christian Faith

Lexham Press, 1313 Commercial St., Bellingham, WA 98225
LexhamPress.com

Print ISBN 9781683593720
Digital ISBN 9781683593737
Library of Congress Control Number 2020930368

Lexham Editorial: Elliot Ritzema, Matthew Boffey, Danielle Thevenaz
Cover Design: Kristen Cork
Typesetting: Abigail Stocker

24 25 26 27 28 29 30 / US / 12 11 10 9 8 7 6 5 4 3 2

Contents

Foreword

SEAN MCDOWELL

"There is good news and there is bad news. Which would you like to hear first?" We've all been asked this question about a host of issues. Personally, I often prefer to hear bad news first to get it out of the way. But I'm going to step out of character and offer the good news first.

Here's the good news: There is a new global generation of young people—often called Generation Z—who are both open to evidence for the Christian faith and who carry less negative baggage about Christians than older generations. In the study *Gen Z* conducted by the Barna Group, nearly half of teens (forty-six percent) say "I need factual evidence to support my beliefs."

And Gen Z'ers in the UK are slightly more positive toward Christian faith and worship than older generations.

For those of us who care about reaching and equipping the next generation, *this is unmistakably good news*! But ...

Here's the bad news: As a church, we are struggling to truly equip young people with answers to the tough questions facing them daily. And we are not engaging non-believing students with both the truth and power of the gospel. As a result, many young Christians disengage from the church and many non-Christians reject Christ.

Given how much is at stake, why aren't we tackling these tough questions head-on?

In my experience, one of the main reasons is because we don't feel equipped. As a church, we really don't know what we believe and why. I often role-play an atheist at camps, conferences, and churches. It's amazing how defensive and aggressive Christian audiences can become. When the role-play is over, I often point out that this is because many people don't know what they believe, and when I press them for answers, they get defensive.

Here's the bottom line: If we are going to equip the next generation of young people and also engage our culture with grace, confidence, and truth, we simply must have answers to the big questions people are asking: *Why*

*is there evil? Is Jesus the only way? Do science and faith con-
flict? Is there a meaning to life?* And so on.

This is why I am thrilled about *Everyday Apologetics*—a
wonderful resource for a number of reasons. Please allow
me to highlight three.

First, this book is accessible. You may have hesitated
to pick up a book with the word "apologetics" in the title.
Apologetics can be intimidating! But each author has gone
to great lengths to tell stories, give understandable illustrations, and make the material accessible.

Second, this book is practical. *Everyday Apologetics* isn't
filled with heady knowledge void of life application. It
deals with scientific and historical issues, but it also deals
with very personal issues like doubt and the meaning of
life. Paul and Chris offer apologetic insights as well as
practical connections to everyday matters.

Third, the authors communicate with kindness. To
try and rise above the distraction in our culture, many
turn to outrage and name-calling. This approach may get
clicks, but it ultimately undermines cultural civility. The
contributors follow the advice of the apostle Paul: "Let
your speech always be gracious, seasoned with salt, so

that you may know how you ought to answer each person" (Colossians 4:6).

This book is a wonderful resource for effective apologetics. I hope you will keep this copy handy, read it, and then put its advice into your everyday life. The *great news* is that God can (and will) use you if you're willing to be used. So go for it!

Introduction: Why Everyday Apologetics?

CHRIS PRICE AND PAUL CHAMBERLAIN

Not too long ago, an eleven-year-old boy I (Chris) know emailed his Christian mother these pointed questions:

"How do Christians get off saying their religion is the only true one?"

"Don't all religions lead to the same God?"

"How do you know there is a God?"

"How can there be a God when there is so much evil and suffering in the world?"

"How can you reconcile belief in God with science and especially evolution?"

"How can you trust the Bible?"

"Why is God so morbidly violent in the Old Testament?"

Pause for a moment and reflect on these objections. How would you answer each one? It feels a little overwhelming, doesn't it? Almost like you need to become an expert in philosophy, biology, history, and theology in order to respond to each concern.

Admittedly, these are not easy issues to tackle and, don't forget, the boy raising these objections was only eleven! For the most part these questions are not new, but as long as new people keep turning up on the planet, fresh answers to age-old questions will be required.

And what *is* new is the easy access provided by the Internet. As Sean McDowell writes, "With the ubiquity of the internet, difficult questions seem to be arising now more than ever."[1] The Internet allows one to readily discover passionate diatribes about the poisonous nature of religion, the absurdity of Christian belief, and the anti-scientific bias of most believers—all with a few simple clicks. This type of continual exposure, much of it sent our way or stumbled upon by accident, can precipitate a crisis of belief for individuals young and old.

Are we prepared? Now more than ever, believers must be.

WHAT IS APOLOGETICS?

Recently I visited the Natural History Museum in London. While we were enjoying the impressive dinosaur exhibit, my host, who didn't identify as a follower of Jesus, asked me whether I believed in dinosaurs. At the time we were both staring at a large, nearly complete dinosaur skeleton, so, needless to say, I was taken aback by her inquiry.

"Sorry, did you ask, 'Do I believe in dinosaurs?'"

(Read with British accent.) "Yeah, quite right. Do you?"

"You mean ... like the one whose remains are standing right in front of me?"

(Host nods head, looks very British.)

"Umm, yes, yes I do."

My host was under the impression that belief in dinosaurs was incompatible with the Christian worldview. I assured her that such was not the case, and even pointed out where the misconception may have arisen.

This interaction forcibly reminded me of the many misleading ideas or cultural objections that people have when it comes to the Christian faith. Every believer has likely encountered similar misunderstandings when watching the news, scrolling through social media feeds, searching the web, or chatting with friends and family about Christianity.

Apologetics helps clear up these misunderstandings. But what does the word *apologetics* actually mean? Many people have heard the term but wonder if it entails learning to apologize for being Christians or, perhaps, attempting to make other people sorry they got into a discussion with us about religion. But the word does not mean "to apologize," at least not in the way we normally experience an apology.

"Apologetics" comes from the Greek word *apologia,* which means "defense." Doing apologetics is speaking in defense of the faith, or providing reasons for belief. It involves untangling the many misconceptions that people lug around due to their upbringing or the various cultural sound bites they've consciously or unconsciously absorbed into their religious point of view. Apologetics serves to clear away the intellectual rubble strewn about by our cultural moment and the entrenched assumptions of our

> "Apologetics" comes from the Greek word *apologia*, which means "defense." Doing apologetics is speaking in defense of the faith, or providing reasons for belief.

day, providing the message of Jesus with a fairer hearing in the marketplace of ideas.

As important as this all sounds, there may be a sliver of suspicion that this whole undertaking is better left to ivory-tower academics or the rare learned person—bookish types, not everyday Christians. We think that is a mistake.

Though we value the contribution of Christian scholars, every Christian is responsible to learn apologetics. Recommending and defending the Christian faith is the duty and (hopefully) delight of believers, who get their marching orders from Jesus in the Great Commission (Matthew 28:16–20). In fact, every Christian will be an apologist for the Christian faith at some point or other. The question is, when that moment comes, will you be well-prepared or poorly equipped?

We wrote *Everyday Apologetics* to help you become a humble and effective advocate for the gospel. We gathered unique voices that are each well versed in navigating the thorny issues and objections people raise to the Christian faith in our cultural context. *Everyday Apologetics* is written for non-experts who are unfamiliar with scholarly language and academic terminology, which is why you'll hear lively stories, anecdotes, and illustrations throughout. There will be clear arguments and easy-to-follow logic, but also some practical tips and applications for everyday Christian living from writers who have a front-row seat to the amazing ways in which God is reaching this post-Christian culture.

In part one, we provide practical advice for how to navigate conversations with skeptics, as well as how to handle personal doubt. In part two, we address common questions and objections to Christianity. In part three, we make a positive case for the truth of the Christian worldview.

In a world of constant change, in a global village where stringent attacks on Christianity are a dime a dozen and a click away, *Everyday Apologetics* strives to be a book in season, useful for churches and individual Christians for such a time as this.

THE NEED FOR EVIDENCE

I (Chris) became a Christian at age twenty, and the only person more surprised by my conversion than my friends was me. In my teen years, I was not a model citizen. I gladly threw myself into a lifestyle of heavy drinking, smoking weed, and, on the odd occasion, snorting cocaine off of my parents' dresser where they kept the family Bible.

Growing up, I had frequented a Southern Baptist congregation with my family. But the distinct odor of irrelevance seemed to cling to the institutional church, making it an unlikely refuge for an insecure, coming-of-age punk. Plus, I heard the church was filled with hypocrites and, frankly, I was proud of the fact that I could forgive myself without the rituals and rigors of conventional religion.

And yet, for a multitude of reasons, unbelief didn't stick with me as I entered my twenties. I know this is not everyone's story and it may even sound a tad cliché, but I felt as though there was a yawning emptiness inside that I couldn't fill with sex, drugs, or alcohol. The bottom dropped out of the fun in my late teens and I was left yearning for something more: meaning, hope, and a deeper purpose for my life. To paraphrase seventeenth-century mathematician and philosopher Blaise Pascal, it is like there was a God-shaped void in my soul that couldn't be filled by any created thing, but only by the Creator. This existential crisis caused me to reexamine my Christian upbringing with a degree of intensity

that I didn't experience growing up. Through a series of
events I was reintroduced to the God of my youth, whom
I hadn't really known. I trusted in Jesus to save me from
my sins and my stubborn, self-centered bent.

Looking back, I am still struck by how I came to
embrace the seemingly hard-to-stomach beliefs of the
Christian faith. For example, that there is one God in three
persons, Father, Son, and Holy Spirit—which requires an
odd, mysterious type of divine arithmetic. That the second
member of the Trinity, God the Son, took on humanity in
Jesus Christ, making him the God/man (a clever name
for a superhero that Marvel has yet to tap). That Jesus
lived the life we should live, without sin, and then died
the death we should die for our sins, making him our
divine benefactor, paying the debts that we alone owe.
That three days later Jesus rose bodily from the dead in
a transformed, physical body, never to die again. That his
resurrection is the linchpin of the Christian faith, apart
from which Christianity is a foolish waste of time.

This is a partial snapshot of the gospel, the most
important news in human history. I believe that what
you believe about this story determines your destiny
and, as such, its truth or falsity is of very real immediate

and infinite importance to us all. C. S. Lewis was on point when he admonished his own generation that "Christianity is a statement which, if false, is of *no* importance, and, if true, of infinite importance. The one thing it cannot be is moderately important."[2] Christianity is of infinite importance, and I believe that is true for me and true for you.

The primary audience for this book is people who subscribe to the Christian faith, people who, upon reading the above paragraphs, are muttering "Amen, Amen." But if you pick up this book unsure about the truth of Christianity, here are a few disclaimers. Though you may presently find the Christian story implausible, and might even harbor a secret suspicion that our Christian faith originates from some sort of gullibility, intellectual deficiency, or refusal to be appropriately skeptical, let me assure you that there are still a lot of things we don't believe.

I don't believe that Elvis or 2Pac rose from the dead and appeared to their devoted fans.

I don't think nature is god. Poison ivy debunked that notion. Or to quote Francis Spufford, "To anyone inclined to think … nature is God, nature replies: have a cup of pus, Mystic Boy."[3] Case closed—at least for me.

I don't believe in the Tooth Fairy—I *am* the Tooth Fairy.

I confess to being an atheist concerning most of the deities dreamed up by the creative imaginings of people (though, admittedly, Thor would be cool to meet).

I don't believe in UFOs.

I have yet to see evidence for a flying teapot orbiting the moon, or the existence of a flying spaghetti monster.

And, for the sake of full disclosure, I refuse to believe that poker is a sport, that non-alcoholic beer is a suitable substitute for the real thing, or that turkey bacon deserves to be called bacon—I suspend belief on all of the above and more.

> I believe Christianity is true on the basis of evidence, and if you are curious about the nature of this evidence, these pages are written for you.

The reason I embrace Christianity and reject the beliefs listed above is largely because of some of the evidence and arguments presented in this book.* You heard right. I believe Christianity is true on the basis of evidence, and if you are curious about the nature of this evidence, these pages are written for you.

---

* For example, see Michael Horner's chapter, "How Fine-Tuning Points Powerfully to God," or Mark Clark's chapter, "The Hope of the Resurrection."

THE NEED FOR ANSWERS

As a young person, my (Paul's) impression of Christianity was rather upbeat. My parents were committed to their Christian faith and modeled it in a positive and consistent manner. Our home was a happy one. We took family vacations, went on boat rides, played sports, and enjoyed countless ice cream treats—a special favorite.

But then one day in my late teens, a serious question entered my mind: How do I know this whole story about God, Jesus, him dying for the sins of the world and rising again, and a few other ideas, is true? I knew we believed all this because we were Christians, but it didn't take a genius to figure out that that alone didn't make it true. What if I'd been raised in a different kind of home, I wondered, say a Muslim or Buddhist one, or even a secular home? I supposed that I would then believe those teachings just as I now believed the Christian ones. But then, why should I believe any of these worldviews at all? I had no interest in believing something just to believe.

I struggled with these thoughts for a few months and found myself unable to find a way to resolve them, so I finally went looking for help. I made an appointment with a respected Christian man in our area, and I'll never forget our short encounter. He welcomed me into his office where I laid out my questions and waited for his answer. And he had one ready to go. With a confident, even radiant, smile, he instructed me to get on my knees and ask God to remove those doubts ... and to stay kneeling until those doubts were gone.

I walked out of that office wondering if this meant there really weren't any answers to my questions. If there were, surely this man would have given me some. It was only later, fortunately not much later, that someone placed in my hands a number of books that I found to be life-changing. Their authors had names like C. S. Lewis, Paul Little, Josh McDowell, and John Warwick Montgomery, and to my amazement they were asking the very questions I was. Even the fact that someone was talking about my questions was profoundly encouraging.

> I began to realize that Christianity had foundations for its core beliefs, and I did not need to kiss my brains goodbye or discard my intellect to embrace it.

As I read, I began to realize that Christianity had foundations for its core beliefs, and I did not need to kiss my brains goodbye or discard my intellect to embrace it. There really are some thoughtful reasons to believe there is a God and that he revealed himself in the person of Jesus of Nazareth who died on a cross for the sins of the world and then rose again from the dead.

I also discovered that searching for reasons to believe these astounding truth claims is not an ill-advised activity. Jesus himself after rising from the dead spent forty days with his disciples, giving them "many convincing proofs" that he had risen from the dead (Acts 1:3). In other words, Jesus was not going to send his disciples out into the world with a message like the one Christianity teaches without arming them with solid reasons to believe it is true. All this was deeply encouraging to me at the time. While not everyone asks the kinds of questions I did, some people do, and this book is intended to provide the kind of help I could have used.

A DISCLAIMER FOR THE SKEPTICAL

Socrates once claimed, "An unexamined life is not worth living." We would add, "An unexamined faith is not worth trusting." Faith means trust or reliance on someone or something. An expanded definition might be that faith is confident trust in what you have good reason to believe. Faith is trust that changes you. And we all exercise faith.

Even the act of thinking requires faith that our reason is reliable and our thoughts actually correspond to reality outside of ourselves.

But keep in mind that Christianity is more like a romance than a puzzle to solve or a hypothesis to be tested in a lab, and we should adjust our expectations for what type of evidence God may provide accordingly.* This is not a cop-out; instead, it is an invitation to know and trust the God who gives enough evidence to convince those whose hearts are open, but not enough evidence to coerce those whose hearts are closed.

> Faith means trust or reliance on someone or something. Faith is trust that changes you.

In the biblical narrative God is a personal being who invites us to know and experience him in a two-way relationship of love. A flaming sword in the sky, or some other type of overwhelming evidence, would do well at producing obedience and grudging submission all around the globe. The problem is this type of brute display of force and power wouldn't produce love. Grudging submission is different than loving surrender, and central to the Christian

---

* Jon Morrison and Michael Horner will discuss these matters more thoroughly in chapters 1 and 8.

story is the belief that God is after the latter. Of course, my having inconvertible evidence that you exist doesn't rob me of a decision about whether or not I want to have a relationship with you.

But God is in a different category than you or me. As the Creator of all things, his presence would overwhelm us, forcing us into a posture of grudging submission or outright rebellion, and we *would* be robbed of our ability to freely choose him. And without this crucial element of free choice there would be no possibility of a genuine, loving relationship, which the Bible tells us God is pursuing.

God woos the soul.

God doesn't force himself on us.

In the end, the contributors to this volume all believe that God gives us enough evidence to surrender our will without surrendering our intellect. We invite you to read the following pages with a charitable frame of mind. Then, in the end, decide for yourself whether the writers succeed in defusing popular objections and making a compelling case for the validity of the Christian worldview.

A FINAL ENCOURAGEMENT

Christians have wrestled with barriers to belief for centuries, and some of the most brilliant thinkers in history have put pen to paper on the matters mentioned in this introduction. Sean McDowell writes:

> The rapidly changing socioeconomic, political, racial, and religious landscape of today's world provides unique challenges. Yet we do not face these challenges in a vacuum. We are standing on the shoulders of giants. Fathers of the church such as Augustine, Aquinas, C. S. Lewis, and Francis Schaeffer have blazed a trail for us to follow.[4]

We are not alone.

Not only do we have access to the power and wisdom of the Holy Spirit, we also have the resources of the entire Christian community throughout history. When we shake off our intellectual apathy and avail ourselves of these resources, loving God with our head, heart, and hands, we rediscover afresh the power of the Christian faith.

> Though the world has changed and will continue to do so, the credibility of the gospel message remains constant.

Though the world has changed and will continue to do so, the credibility of the gospel message remains constant.

People are still beautiful.

People are still broken.

People are still longing for love, hope, and meaning. People still ache somewhere deep in their bones for redemption and new life.

The gospel of Jesus Christ is still the only hope for this tired, misbehaving planet and the people who populate its surface, and we must be prepared to both defend and commend this beautiful message in our information-saturated, postmodern world.

So take and read this work for what it is. We sincerely hope it is helpful. But our final caution is this: don't mistake our arguments for the reality, because God can only be truly *known* through the person of Jesus. The realness of the risen Christ can be encountered in the here and now, and this book is meant to point beyond itself to the God who loved us and gave himself up for us. May Jesus get the glory, may you experience his joy, and may all people revel in the hope that is ultimately and always found only in him—a hope that is intellectually credible and emotionally satisfying.

Part 1

Defending the Faith Today

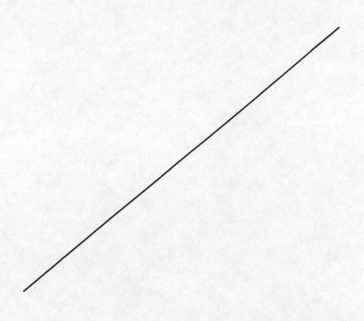

1. The Nagging Doubts That Strengthened My Faith

JON MORRISON

Too many followers of Jesus seem to be losing their confidence in the truth of Christianity. While they want to have a confident, vibrant faith and share with others about it, they do not know how to deal with doubts. Doubt can feel like a sin you must keep secret because you will be called "rebellious" or "too critical."

My first ministry job was as a youth pastor in a suburb of Vancouver, British Columbia. On the West Coast, in a post-Christian culture in which the number of Christians and knowledge of the Christian worldview have declined, less than five percent of the population will be in church on a Sunday. Every week at youth group I would face an onslaught of tough questions from skeptical students.

And the truth is, the students' questions exposed my own questions about my faith. In Bible school, I don't remember any class ever addressing questions about the trustworthiness of Scripture or the potential conflict between faith and science or the issue of evil and suffering—the very questions that students would raise on a weekly basis. My professors talked about how to preach through the book of Romans and discussed various theories about who wrote the book of Hebrews, but we never engaged with philosophy or the sciences, and I was never offered a single class in Christian apologetics. As a result, I didn't have all the tools I needed for ministry in a post-Christian context.

> I used to think that doubt was always a bad thing. Now I see that doubt can be the starting point for a stronger walk with God.

There is a passage in the book of Hosea where God laments, "My people are destroyed from lack of knowledge" (Hosea 4:6). In other words, ignorance comes with a price tag, and I nearly paid in full. My inability to reason through my doubts could have cost me my career and everything that I had built my life on up to that point.

During this season, my confidence in the truth of Christianity began to erode. At first, it was just a few pebbles and some dirt that fell away. Then the whole embankment on which I had built my life felt like it was collapsing. I wondered whether I was living a lie. Even worse, I asked myself whether I was one of those frauds leading others into a false religion.

If Christianity was a lie, I was a huckster. The thought terrified me.

Some people can get stuck in doubt for a season, but I couldn't afford to stay stuck. There was too much at stake. I had to go to work each day and talk about my faith. I had to write sermons and counsel youth. I was an ambassador for the truth of Christianity. Like a wet shirt that you just can't get off, I had to fight and wiggle and do whatever it took to remove the cloak of doubt that clung to me.

I used to think that doubt was always a bad thing. Now I see that doubt can be the starting point for a stronger walk with God. After having gone through my own season of doubt, I have emerged more convinced than ever that Christianity is true and that everyone needs to know how amazing it is to have a relationship with Jesus.

WHAT KIND OF DOUBTER ARE YOU?

Early on in my journey of dealing with doubt I discovered a well-known Christian scholar, Gary Habermas, who struggled with doubt and had written extensively about it. His book *Dealing with Doubt* gave me some language that helped me understand the different kinds of doubt. He writes about three categories of doubts: emotional, volitional, and logical.[1]

Emotional doubts arise when something throws off your emotional balance. A bad breakup, a sickness, a death in the family, or an unanswered prayer can lead to emotional doubt. When we doubt emotionally, we don't like God. We are more frustrated with him than anything. Our questions end with exclamation marks.

Emotions are part of being human. We experience highs and lows. In the lows, we can doubt God ... or anything. Maturity means being able to overcome emotional doubts. C. S. Lewis writes in *Mere Christianity*, "Now Faith ...

> Faith is holding onto what you believed when you were thinking straight.

is the art of holding on to things your reason has once accepted, in spite of your changing moods. For moods will change, whatever view your reason takes. I know that by experience."[2]

Faith is holding onto what you believed when you were thinking straight. If you remember this, you can talk yourself out of emotional doubts. Why? Because you already know what is right; you are just questioning it because of some unexpected or difficult circumstances. To get out of emotional doubt, you exercise your will to overpower your emotions. This was the approach of the writer of Psalm 42, who says to his soul, "Why are you cast down, O my soul, and why are you in turmoil within me?" Here he is speaking to his weary soul. And his follow-up to his first question is what will get him out of his emotional rut: "Hope in God; for I shall again praise him, my salvation and my God" (Ps 42:11 ESV).

Volitional doubts, unlike emotional doubts, engage the will first. You begin by not wanting something to be true, and so you intentionally begin to doubt, hoping that what you find in your research will confirm your initial desire to reject the belief in question.

There are times in our lives when we would like Christianity to not be true. Perhaps it is on a Friday when our hearts want to join our friends who are doing something we know the Bible would never condone. Our fleshly desires scream out at us, "This stuff can't be true!" We know that it is not logic or reason making such claims. We just want to join in the "fun" for a while, and one of the easiest ways to get around our conscience is to deny our faith.

We also doubt volitionally when the offering is announced at church and we daydream about all the other things we could do with that tithe money. Our sin nature would rather we give to ourselves than to God, and so we try to reason why it could be better to keep the money rather than doing what we know God wants.

If we are honest, this is a constant struggle in most of us. The volitional doubter is summed up admirably by the words a character speaks in Marilynne Robinson's novel *Gilead*: "It seems to me some people just go around looking to get their faith unsettled. That has been the fashion for the last hundred years or so."[3]

Logical doubts are brought about by a crisis of information. Our ignorance about a certain topic leads to great uncertainty, unsettling our convictions. We deal with logical doubts by doing research. We read books. We consider ideas. We attend lectures. We invest diligently in acquiring more knowledge. Then we have to sift through it all and see what makes the most sense. We have to ask, What is consistent? What view lines up with how the world seems to work? Many logical doubts are cured with some research, clear thinking, and good old-fashioned reason.

As I reflected on my own doubts, I found that they were mostly logical in nature. This meant that the solution for me was more study—a desire that led to big changes in my life.

The changes began when my roommate was listening to a podcast by Christian apologist Ravi Zacharias. In it, he was discussing a program at Oxford University dedicated to equipping young leaders to answer the tough questions of life.[4] My roommate walked in the door after work and declared, "Jon, you need to go study at Oxford. I think it will help you."

He was right. I did need to go. But for a kid who grew up in a hockey dressing room and earned a straight "B" average in high school, Oxford was never on my radar. And yet, I somehow knew my roommate's crazy idea was actually a nudge from God. I resigned from my youth pastor job and sold all my possessions, even my beloved motorcycle, keeping only what I could fit into a suitcase. I walked away from everything so I could learn how to settle my doubts.

WHEN DOUBT IS A GOOD THING

Andrea Lucado is a Christian writer who was raised in the church and also emerged from a season of doubt. Looking back on her experience, she notes that the struggling, wrestling, and questioning were all part of her discipleship experience. Lucado concluded that her doubt was not the absence of having faith, but in fact the first step toward having real faith.[5] I found the same thing to be true in my own life.

In this way, doubt can be a good thing—an invitation to a stronger, more robust faith. A while ago I was speaking at a camp for high school students, and a student approached me after an emotional campfire night. This teenager was struggling with his doubts about God. He said he was on the brink of walking away from God and wanted some help.

"That god you just described is not the God of the Bible, so you were good to doubt him."

I asked him to describe the kind of God he was walking away from. He described a deity that was always angry with him: unkind, uninvolved in the world, and uncaring toward the poor and marginalized. I told him that he should reject that god as soon as possible, and that I had already dismissed that god long ago: "That god you just described is not the God of the Bible, so you were good to doubt him. Now you need to learn about what the Bible says God is really like."

Here's another example of how doubt can be a good thing. Several years ago, I owned a car with a faulty gas gauge. I knew it was faulty because it read as full no matter how much I drove. Having had this car for a while, I knew how far I could go between fill-ups. One time I pushed it a little too far. The gauge read "Full," but I was pretty sure I was running on fumes. Rather than being confident in the faulty dial, I doubted what I was reading and went to the gas station.

> Sometimes, if you are wrong about something, the best thing to do is doubt. Doubt can be a stepping-stone on your way to a greater understanding of the truth.

Thank goodness I did! The tank was empty. Had I gone on any longer, I would have had to make that walk of shame along the side of the road, gas can in hand.

Sometimes, if you are wrong about something, the best thing to do is doubt. Doubt can be a stepping-stone

on your way to a greater understanding of the truth.
Doubt can be helpful, but there are three words doubters often hear that are not helpful at all.

THREE OF THE MOST
UNHELPFUL WORDS

"Just have faith" are words that no one wants to hear in
the middle of doubt. Telling a doubter this is like telling
a man dying of thirst in the desert to "just drink water."
Faith is the problem for the one clouded by uncertainty.
Can you just produce faith by trying harder, digging
deeper, or clinging on tighter? I don't think so, because
faith is not what many people assume.

According to some critics of Christianity, faith is belief
without evidence, a leap in the dark despite your better
judgment. Atheist Richard Dawkins sums this up well:
"Faith is the great cop-out, the great excuse to evade the
need to think and evaluate evidence. Faith is the belief in
spite of, even perhaps because of, the lack of evidence."[6]
It is hard to know where Dawkins gets this definition
of faith, because Christians don't believe faith means
believing in something without evidence. Likewise, it

isn't "believing what you know ain't so," as Mark Twain once quipped.[7]

My friend and one of the contributors to this book, Andy Steiger, defines faith as "trusting in what we have good evidence to believe." Faith in the New Testament is based on responding to evidence. Jesus, in John 14, suggested that people should believe in him because they could see the miracles he was doing. At the end of John's Gospel, we find John's thesis statement: "These are written so that you may believe that Jesus is the Christ, the Son of God, and that by believing you may have life in his name" (John 20:31 ESV). John has just written twenty chapters highlighting Jesus' miracles and teaching, and then says (I'll paraphrase), "I wrote all this down so you will be able to make an educated decision about Jesus and trust in him for eternal life."

Luke does the same thing at the beginning of his Gospel. He lets us know the main point of his writing: "It seemed good to me also, having followed all things closely for some time past, to write an orderly account for you, most excellent Theophilus, by which you may have certainty concerning the things you have been taught" (Luke 1:3–4 ESV).

Does this sound like someone advocating blind belief? Not at all! In fact, it is the opposite. The Bible encourages us to have faith and trust in Jesus based on what we have seen and read and thought through.

Oswald Chambers, the late Scottish pastor and writer, encouraged his readers to wrestle their beliefs to the ground and, in the process, make their faith their own. He writes in his classic devotional, *My Utmost for His Highest*, "Always make it a practice to stir your mind thoroughly to think through what you have accepted. Your position is not yours until you make it yours through suffering and study."[8]

> To tell a person in doubt to "just have faith" is advocating for blind belief, but blind belief has no place in the Christian tradition.

To tell a person in doubt to "just have faith" is advocating for blind belief, but blind belief has no place in the Christian tradition. Followers of Jesus should develop a thoughtful faith and thoroughly consider their beliefs. And the good news is that you can do all of this thinking when you're in the middle of a season of doubt. Doubt doesn't prevent you from doing the research and working your way through the core beliefs of Christianity. The end result can be a stronger faith.

But that is not always the case, because doubt is not static. Doubt is a verb; it is a "doing" word. Doubt doesn't stand still; it moves us along a path either toward God or away from God. And it is in the movement away from God that we experience the dark side of doubt.

THE DARK SIDE OF DOUBT

Sean became a friend during my time studying at Oxford. I was keen to talk about philosophical topics, and he was happy to oblige and share his reasons for not being a Christian. Though Sean grew up going to church, he had walked away from his parents' faith, claiming to have too many doubts. Each time we met, many months apart, I would ask him what he was doing about his doubt.

"Not much," was his answer. He hadn't looked at the books I recommended or watched the videos I had sent him. Sean, a volitional doubter, was refusing to pursue truth. Instead, he wore his doubt like a badge of honor.

Like Sean, volitional doubters I have met often transition from initial doubt, which is not a sin, toward the sin of unbelief. The sin of unbelief is a choice to remain in doubt and skepticism rather than to seek the truth with an open heart and mind.

Instead of saying "Help my unbelief" (Mark 9:24), this posture of the heart refuses to pray because to pray may open up the door again to belief. To open one's mind may lead to an opening of one's heart, and that is too risky. The sin of unbelief is an arms-crossed, back-turned posture toward God. This is the dark side of doubt.

Doubt is not neutral—it can slide into the sin of unbelief if we do not take steps to address our doubts. Thankfully, by God's grace, even in the deepest darkness there is always some light to guide us back to a confident trust in the person of Christ and the truth of Christianity.

MOVING FROM DOUBT TO FAITH

How can you emerge from a season of doubt with a stronger faith? Here are four pieces of advice that will help you to actively move through doubt toward a growing faith that is both thoughtful and sincere.

1. REMEMBER THAT GOD WELCOMES US WITH OUR DOUBTS.

Nowhere in the Bible are doubts discouraged or condemned. The disciple Thomas is an excellent case study of someone who was struggling with doubt and was welcomed by Jesus. After some of the other disciples had seen the risen Christ and reported to Thomas that Jesus was no longer dead but alive, Thomas responded initially with skepticism. He was not one to just accept miracle claims without evidence. In a statement that earned him his nickname, "Doubting Thomas," he exclaimed, "Unless I see the nail marks in his hands and put my finger where the nails were, and put my hand into his side, I will not believe" (John 20:25)! Eight days later, his desires were fulfilled. Jesus appeared in the crowded room and singled Thomas out. Jesus invited Thomas to touch his nail-scarred hands and believe in the reality of the resurrection.

> Nowhere in the Bible are doubts discouraged or condemned.

Let us not miss the fact that Jesus does not sound angry in this story. He does not ignore Thomas. He does not condemn him—quite the opposite. He tenderly engages his struggling disciple and offers him the desires of his heart: evidence to believe. And Thomas' response is the right one when presented with evidence of the truth: "Thomas said to him, 'My Lord and my God!'" (John 20:28).

This story comforts me. Jesus is not against those who struggle with doubt. In the book of Jude, God's word says explicitly, "Be merciful to those who doubt" (Jude 1:22), and we see that in the character of Jesus. He is for us and he meets us in our questioning with love, mercy, and compassion.

2. WATCH YOUR EXPECTATIONS.

A lot of doubt comes from unmet expectations. I confess that some of my struggle with God was not just intellectual. I was mad at God because I didn't get my way enough. When selfish human beings do not get our way, we get mad. When we get mad, we start making unjust, unreasonable demands.

I have heard many say, "If God would just show up here right beside me, I wouldn't doubt anymore." I doubt that is the case.

This demand is unreasonable for many reasons, but I will name just two. One, if God, the Creator of the universe, showed up beside you in all his glory, you would not be around anymore to contemplate your level of faith. Your finite, frail body would not be able to handle the sheer power of his presence. As God says to Moses, "No one may see me and live" (Exodus 33:20). We must be careful what we demand of an all-powerful and good God.

The second reason I don't think that God showing up beside us creates belief is that when God did veil his power and glory to come and draw near us in Jesus, people still did not believe. In the stories about Jesus' life in the Gospels, people denied him all the time. They didn't accept what he said, and his miracles were not sufficient to create belief—not even for his family members (see John 7:5). In fact, even Jesus' resurrection wasn't enough for some. Matthew 28:17 says of his disciples, "When they saw him, they worshiped him; but some doubted." Still doubted? Really? How is that possible? I suppose unless I was there, I cannot judge. And if I were there, perhaps I would have doubted, too. Clearly, having Jesus standing right beside you is still not enough evidence to create or compel belief.

John the Baptizer was a man who struggled with doubt because of his misguided expectations. In the Gospels, John presented Jesus as "the Lamb of God, who takes away the sin of the world" (John 1:29). And when John baptized Jesus it was a moving event. The Bible says "heaven was opened, and he saw the Spirit of God descending like a dove and alighting on him. And a voice from heaven said, 'This is my Son, whom I love; with him I am well pleased'" (Matthew 3:16–17). John witnessed all of this, and we can assume his belief in Jesus as the Son of God was firm. His original expectations of what Jesus would do, however, would eventually create doubt in his heart.

John was imprisoned for calling out the ruler Herod Antipas for his adulterous lifestyle. While sitting alone in prison, questions began to arise in John's mind: If my cousin, Jesus, were the Messiah, why would he allow me to remain in this prison? How does Herod still have any power over me? I'm related to the one who is supposed to be overthrowing the entire empire!

You see, John, like most first-century Jewish people, knew the Old Testament well. He had studied all the passages about what the promised king would do, so he waited in eager anticipation for Jesus to begin the process of cleaning up the mess that was the nation of Israel. John would have believed that the Messiah was destined to lead Israel to countless military victories, ushering in a return to the golden age of Israel when their enemies would be defeated—that the messianic king would reclaim David's throne. Instead, God's enemies continued to flourish, and the would-be Messiah seemed indifferent to John's suffering in prison. As a result, John started to entertain doubts about whether Jesus was indeed the promised Messiah. John eventually sent some of his followers over to Jesus to see what was going on. They asked Jesus, "Are you the one who is to come, or should we expect someone else?" (Matthew 11:3).

Freedom was John's expectation. The prison was his experience. Doubt was the outcome.

I love how Jesus responded. Note that he doesn't say what many of our Christian family members might tell those of us struggling with doubt. Jesus doesn't utter the dreaded line, "Tell John to just have faith!" Rather, Jesus says, "Go back and report to John what you hear and see: The blind receive sight, the lame walk, those who have leprosy are cleansed, the deaf hear, the dead are raised, and the good news is proclaimed to the poor" (Matthew 11:4–5).

Jesus gives evidence for faith. But that is not all Jesus said. He then adds this line that rings true to all of us whose unmet expectations of God have led us to doubt him: "Blessed is anyone who does not stumble on account of me" (Matthew 11:6). Theologian D. A. Carson translates this comment to mean that the one who is blessed by God "does not find in [Jesus] and his ministry an obstacle to belief and therefore reject him."[9] Carson says that you are blessed when you do not find Jesus' works (or seeming lack thereof) as an obstacle or deal breaker to your trust in him.

> In faith, you settle in your heart that God is good and all he does is good. That is how you deal with doubt caused by unmet expectations.

Rather than taking offense when he doesn't do something you want, you submit and trust. In faith, you settle in your heart that God is good and all he does is good. That is how you deal with doubt caused by unmet expectations.

3. REMEMBER GOD'S CHARACTER.

Dr. Gary Habermas, whose book about doubt I mentioned earlier, has become a trusted friend of mine over the last couple of years. He has spoken to me at length about his own years of doubt after his wife died of cancer. When I asked Gary why such a tragic loss did not ultimately shake his confidence in God, he said something very memorable: that he had previously learned to trust God intellectually, but during that time he also learned to trust God's character relationally.

In other words, Gary had learned enough about the nature of God and how he works that when there was something that confused him or caused him to question God, he had learned to trust him. During an interview I conducted with him, he said, "I have learned to trust God for the things I do know about him when I am challenged with the things I don't."

In the twenty-first century, we have plenty of reasons to believe that God is good. We have the stories of how he worked in the lives of the biblical characters; we have the death and resurrection of Jesus, a display of God's love, grace, and power; we have the testimony of church history; and, finally, we have our personal experiences of times when God has helped us. All of these, according to Habermas, are faith-building moments in the past that help assure us about the goodness of God's character when we are feeling confused or experiencing doubt in the present.

4. FIND A SUPPORT NETWORK.

Doubt can feel lonely. But I hope this chapter has helped you see that doubt is more common than we sometimes think. Most Christians go through a season of doubt at some point, and it is important to realize that you are not alone.

It is important to find people who will walk through doubt with you. Does anyone know you are struggling? Sometimes it takes a bit of courage to let other people know how you are doing. It may mean giving up a night or two of your week and signing up to be a part of a small group or even a program like Alpha where you can wrestle through some of your questions.[10] These are groups that are designed to let people air out their questions in an environment that is inviting and safe.

> Most Christians go through a season of doubt at some point, and it is important to realize that you are not alone.

Maybe you are in a small town or an isolated spot where there is no one around to whom you can talk. The good news is that we live in an age where technology connects people from all around the world. Do you have access to the internet? There are all kinds of websites and groups available for those who are struggling with doubt or wrestling with the truth claims of Christianity.

There is even a society for sea kayakers who wear red hats on Thursday.

You will find a place to fit in.

CONCLUSION

While my journey continues today, a critical point that in many ways acted as a conclusion to my season of doubting was a formal, public debate that I was a part of in November of 2015. A large network of atheists was having a conference, and they wanted to engage a Christian apologist as the finale to the event.

I was asked to debate Matt Dillahunty, a well-known skeptic from Dallas, Texas. The debate was a moment when I knew that something was different in me. I stood there in front of hundreds of atheists and one professional skeptic and held my ground. There was no question that stumped me and no accusation that rattled my faith.[11]

God led me on a sacred path called "doubt," and on the way I was given training by some of the best thinkers in the world. While doubts can always come back, I am more confident than ever that I have learned the right tools to help me deal with them.

While you may not be asked to engage a professional skeptic, sometimes there is no louder voice than the skeptic that can reside in your own heart. But be encouraged, because doubt is normal.

And, thankfully, it is also curable.

2. Responding to a New Kind of Skeptic

PAUL CHAMBERLAIN

Some time ago, I and my colleague Michael Horner (one of the other contributors to this book) were invited to participate in a public debate with two atheists. This was not a garden-variety debate; it was to be the opening act of an atheist convention attended by a few hundred atheists from around North America, and even a few from overseas. In a strange sort of way, I felt honored to be asked. We readily accepted and began our preparations.

When I mentioned this upcoming event to others, one particular question kept coming up among both Christians and people of no faith, usually accompanied by a shrug of the shoulders: *Why would atheists have a convention?* As one person put it wryly, "What are they celebrating? Nothingness?" I found the question amusing and said I would try to find out.

Once I arrived at the conference, the answer quickly became obvious. The vast majority of those in attendance did not merely believe there was no God; they were former members of some religious group from which they had been "set free," and they were now celebrating their liberated status as atheists. The theme of the conference was "Imagine No Religion." One of the debaters we engaged was a former Southern Baptist who had been preparing for ministry; the other had been a Catholic altar boy. Others were former Jehovah's Witnesses, Mormons, Muslims, and the like.

This conference exemplifies something different happening in the world of faith and religion in the Western world. There has emerged a new and passionate kind of skeptic—one who, in the past, was a devout member of the Christian community, who worshiped alongside the rest of us. These skeptics prayed and read their Bibles and believed what they read. Some, in fact, were leaders in the Christian community: pastors, professors, theologians, authors, church planters, and theology students.

These new skeptics are being supported by a growing number of organizations—usually web-based—devoted to helping and encouraging them in their journey away from the faith. One, The Clergy Project (TCP), exists to "provide a safe haven of protected, anonymous online community for former and active religious professionals who no longer hold to supernatural beliefs."[1] Another, Christians Anonymous (CA), proclaims itself to be "a resource for recovering Christians." CA sets out its own twelve-step program, patterned after Alcoholics Anonymous, to help people become free from the "mental enslavement" that comes from "the addiction of Christianity," which it calls a "disease of the mind."[2]

> Conversations with these new skeptics will be different from conversations with skeptics who have never been part of the Christian community.

A DIFFERENT TAKE ON CHRISTIANITY

Conversations with these new skeptics will be different from conversations with skeptics who have never been part of the Christian community. They do not need to be told what it's like to be a Christian. In some cases, they know their Bibles, their theology, and their history of Christianity better than many Christians do.

Many of them have also honed their skills in presenting their case against Christianity. If you ask them to take some teachings by faith, they are unlikely to go along. More likely, they'll ask you if you offer the same concession to people of other faiths when their teachings run into difficulties. Most importantly, the objections they raise against Christianity are not likely to be ones most Christians have thought about. They've heard the typical arguments, have found them inadequate, and have concluded that there aren't any good ones. It's why they left. Often, their goal is to persuade other Christians to join them in their rejection of Christianity, or at least to provide a safe haven for Christians who become disillusioned with their faith.

Their knowledge of common arguments in favor of Christianity can be unsettling for someone who wants to talk with them about faith. For example, a friend of mine whom I'll call Steve had read and studied the Bible more than most Christians both in college and on his own. He was active in his church and had gone on to be a respected professional in his field. One of his work colleagues had once been a devout Christian but had rejected the faith and was now an ardent and, as it turned out, very knowledgeable skeptic of Christianity. Steve and this colleague were asked by their company to travel to a different city for a weekend and take care of a project together. Steve saw it as a golden opportunity to share the message of Jesus with him. Perhaps he could encourage him to reconsider his decision to turn away from his faith. He asked his church friends to pray for him, and off they went.

Things did not go according to plan—at least, not Steve's plan. The colleague was no passive recipient and, like Steve, welcomed the opportunity to present his case. The weekend turned into a bruising encounter in which Steve's attempts to share his faith were frustrated by a well-prepared skeptic.

Every time Steve made a point, his colleague seemed to be one step ahead of him. He knew the point and immediately raised a problem with it. In most cases, Steve found himself unable to respond. And when Steve was through, his colleague started in, raising new challenges Steve had not thought of. The longer it went, the worse it got. Where was God, Steve wondered, when he really needed him? Didn't Jesus say in Luke 21:15 that he would give us words to say when tough questions were thrown our way?

My hat is off to people like Steve. They don't keep their heads down; they take up the challenge, and the privilege, of sharing the message of Jesus with skeptics like these. This chapter is an encouragement to all of us to do the same. I'll return to Steve's story later, but for now let me ask: How can we better our efforts to share our faith with this new kind of skeptic? I have found the following seven principles to be helpful. They can be used in conversations with any kind of skeptic, but they are especially helpful with a skeptic who has rejected Christianity. I encourage you to consider these and then see if there are others you might add to the list.

1. ACKNOWLEDGE SKEPTICS' REASONS FOR WHY THEY TURNED AWAY

I was once at a gathering with a skeptic who had rejected his faith and no longer wanted anything to do with the church or Christianity. His every mention of God or

Christianity was in the form of a dig or a joke. At one point, someone hinted that something other than intellectual objections must have caused him to leave the faith and wondered aloud what the real reason might be. In this person's mind, there just had to be other factors than the ones he was mentioning. Another person went further and suggested that perhaps he had not searched hard enough for answers or for Jesus because, if he would have, surely he would have found those answers. After all, didn't God even say that if people search for him with their whole hearts they would find him (Jeremiah 29:13)?

Suddenly all joking was left aside. "Frankly, I find that offensive," the skeptic fired back. "Just how would you know that I didn't look hard enough for answers or do my homework?" He understood the thinking that was behind those comments because he used to think that way himself. Then he added: "Your problem is that you just can't imagine anyone finding problems with the things you believe." As far as this skeptic was concerned, he was not being taken seriously. These Christians were finding an easy way to write off his decision as the result of laziness or emotional causes.

It may be our natural tendency to dismiss a skeptic's objections and assume there are other factors at work. There are at least two reasons to avoid this approach. First, all of us like to be taken seriously when we say why we were driven to a certain action, and this includes skeptics who tell us why they left the faith. When we suggest there must be other reasons, it implies that we somehow know more than they do about what was behind their decision, that somehow our reasons are so good, and theirs so weak, that surely there must be other factors at work. Just put yourself in the shoes of the skeptic for a minute and you'll see how offensive that could come across.

This is not to deny that there may be other factors. I know of cases in which there actually were moral failings, disappointments with the church, opposition from other Christians when trying to do good, and so on. But I also know of cases where no such other factors jump out. Let's remember that if there do happen to be other reasons, it still doesn't invalidate the reasons skeptics give. I would encourage you to begin the discussion there.

The second reason to avoid this approach is even more important. Setting aside the reasons skeptics give and searching for "the real reasons" can come across as nothing more than an attempt to avoid dealing with their reasons for turning away from Christianity. They may well respond like the skeptic above: "You just don't want to deal with the reasons I am giving you for why I couldn't believe this stuff anymore." If we appear to be taking the easy route of not engaging their reasons, it's hard to think we'll earn the right to learn about any other factors that may have influenced their decision to leave.

If we appear to be taking the easy route of not engaging their reasons, it's hard to think we'll earn the right to learn about any other factors that may have influenced their decision to leave.

2. REMEMBER THE SKEPTIC IS NOT THE ENEMY

I was once introduced to a young man who had grown up a Christian but was now making it well known that he was an atheist and ready to defend his new position. After I exchanged greetings with the young man, I was asked by a third person, "Did you just shake hands with the enemy?"

Maybe you've met people who have turned away from the Jesus they once worshiped. How do we view such people? Do we think of them as having gone over to the dark side, or joined the enemy, or even *become* the enemy? What if they come across as particularly aggressive or even hostile?

After giving a lecture on Christianity at a local public university, I was immediately accosted by a young man surrounded by a group of friends. Perhaps *accosted* is the wrong word (after all I had just invited people to come for further conversation), but if you'd been there, you would know why I use it. He didn't just walk forward; he *strode*. And when he got to me, he loudly proclaimed that there were two things he hated: philosophy and Christianity. Since my own doctoral studies were in philosophy and I was there representing Christianity, he had me on both counts.

"What are you into?" I asked.

"Science," he said flatly. "And what's more," he went on, "using science, I could disprove Christianity in five minutes."

"That's quite a promise," I replied, and told him to go ahead and take his best shot. He proceeded to set out two arguments that he believed were decisive against Christianity, and I followed by asking him questions about his reasoning. Twenty minutes later, we parted company after a conversation that, fortunately, had turned increasingly civil and productive.

On another occasion, at the end of a public debate I was involved in, we moved to questions from the audience. Most people were thoughtful and respectful, with some even injecting humor, but then one questioner rose and angrily denounced my position. He was agitated and waving his arms to the point that I began to wonder whether he might have taken a swing at me if he had been close enough. Fortunately, he was near the back of a fairly large room. As he went on, it was obvious he was deeply opposed to what I had promoted for personal reasons that had affected his own family—reasons that he explained to me and an entire room full of people.

As I watched and listened to both of these skeptics, it was tempting to view them as enemies. They were aggressive and loud—one was highly agitated—and they were intent on disproving the message I had just represented. But they were not enemies. If there is an enemy in this business, it is the one Peter describes as our adversary who is prowling around like a roaring lion looking for someone to devour (1 Peter 5:8). It's a vivid picture of the devil. The skeptics we talk to, however, are simply people like us, creations of a loving God who is reaching out to them and, in fact, using us to do so. Their loud or aggressive attitudes do not turn them into the enemy. They only show the passion with which they hold their views. So long as they are willing to speak with us, we should take the opportunities to engage them thoughtfully and graciously.

Remembering this principle can change the way we respond and communicate the message of Jesus to the new kind of skeptic. Rather than view them as enemies, we need to recognize that something caused their passionate stance. People have experiences in life and some lead to resentment, disappointment, or even anger with God. Writing skeptics off as enemies achieves nothing and, in fact, may be a cop-out on our part. Our goal should be to ask further questions once we have earned the right to do so. Who knows? We may be given the chance to discuss the very real issues or experiences that are producing this attitude. Maybe we can't solve it, but at least we can build a bridge and have a respectful conversation. It's all part of the longer process through which God draws people to himself, and we get to be part of that.

3. DON'T GET SIDETRACKED

Perhaps you've had the experience of inviting someone to tell you why they no longer believe, or maybe why they never have, only to hear not just one, or two, or even three challenges to Christianity, but a whole series of them bundled together in one confusing package. There is a good chance the challenges were also interspersed with a few emotionally charged stories. If so, welcome to the world of sorting through the messiness of people's reasons for rejecting the faith.

Once, when I was speaking to a group of young people consisting of both Christians and non-Christians, we decided to devote the majority of the time to addressing questions they had about Christianity. At one point, a college student stood and asked a question that stands out in my mind to this day. He said his mother had recently died and, while she had been a kind and compassionate person, she had never been a follower of Jesus. Does that mean, he asked pointedly, that she is in hell today?

If you have engaged people about Christianity much at all, you will also have encountered this question. It is often asked very passionately. After all, this is the person's mother they are talking about. What should we say, "Yes, that's exactly what I'm saying; next question please." Obviously not. But if that is a bad answer, what is a better one? I know of no way to win over that person or advance that conversation by answering "yes" or "no." However, we also do not want to come across as trying to evade tough questions.

My answer to the young man was drawn from a discussion I had a few years before with Ravi Zacharias, an experienced and wise Christian apologist who was asked this exact question. Ravi replied with the following answer, and it's the one I also gave that evening:

> I want to honor your mother for her good life of kindness to others. And I cannot say where your mother is right now because I do not know what business she may have done with God either during her life or at the end of life. However, the most important thing I can tell you today is that Christ died so that we can spend eternity with him.[3]

This answer does four things, and it is why I continue to use it in my own discussions:

- It does not evade the issue.

- It does not say more than we can or should. None of us knows with certainty where that mother is at this moment. That is information to which we are not privy.

- It honors a person for a life of kindness and compassion; why would we want to avoid doing that?

- It brings the conversation back to the important truth that Christ died so people could be reconciled to him. As messengers of Christ, this is the most important message we have to communicate and we should continually return to it.

As I noted earlier, sometimes people's reasons for rejecting the faith can actually be a complex of intellectual arguments and emotional reactions. We've all had the experience of talking in circles and seemingly getting nowhere. This principle can help us. My own approach is often to say, "You've said a lot of things here. I'm not sure about you, but I'm a lot better at this when I focus on one thing at a time." You will, no doubt, have your own way of putting it, but it allows you to face a question head on and search for a way to return to the big ideas of Christianity, the ones we really hope the person will eventually embrace.

> My own approach is often to say, "You've said a lot of things here. I'm not sure about you, but I'm a lot better at this when I focus on one thing at a time."

4. DISTINGUISH CHRISTIANITY FROM THE ABUSE OF CHRISTIANITY

I was participating in a public dialogue on a university campus some time ago with an atheist professor who had been raised a Christian but later turned from his faith. At one point he turned to me and said that one reason he could never believe in God again was because this belief obviously did not make people good; in fact, it might even make them bad, or at least worse than they would be otherwise.

I wondered where he was going with this point but didn't have to wait long to find out. He immediately supported it by calling the audience's attention to abortion clinic bombers who often say God told them to do it. Of course, God had done no such thing, said the professor, because there was no God, but this showed that the belief in God could turn a person into someone willing to blow up a medical building and kill everyone inside.

But he didn't stop there. He went on to list the actions of certain televangelists who had misused their power and positions and done egregious things, including asking for money from poor elderly people to support their own opulent lifestyle, all while believing in God. Their belief in God had not made them good, he repeated. Quite the opposite. And then there are the religious leaders who, in times past, burned people at the stake because their doctrine "wasn't quite right." By the time he was done, belief in God had been turned into something ugly and violent that no peace-loving person would want to embrace.

How might you reply to this challenge? When it was time for me to respond, I remembered something I had learned from one of my professors. We need to make a distinction, he had said, between what some people have done in the name of God or Christianity on the one hand,

and what Jesus or the Bible really teach on the other.[4] We are called to defend the second but not the first.

So in response, I made the following comment: "You are not the only one here who condemns these actions. I do, too, maybe even more strongly than you because of how it blackens the name of the Jesus I follow. But what these people did does not show that Christianity is false or violent or any such thing. While they may have been claiming to act in the name of Christianity or God, the fact is their actions actually violated the teachings of our founder, Jesus. He called his followers to love their enemies, turn the other cheek, pray for those who perse-cute them, and do unto others as they would have them do unto them."

> The fact that someone has abused a belief system or ideal is never a good reason on its own to reject that belief system.

This is an answer I've now given many times over the years. It's powerful because it rests on a key princi-ple, namely that we should not judge something by its abuse. With just a moment's thought, we all know this to be true as well. The fact that someone has abused a belief system or ideal is never a good reason on its own to reject that belief system. Throughout human history, horrific actions have been performed in the name of such ideals as patriotism, nationalism, ethnicity, liberty, equality, fraternity, atheism, religion, and many others. All of these ideals have been taken to extremes or abused in a variety of ways, but such abuse alone does not constitute a reason to reject them. Christianity, too, has been abused by those claiming to be Christians, and this means we must be prepared to defend genuine Christian teaching but not necessarily every action performed in the name of Christianity.

Whenever someone complains of the wars caused by Christianity, or even ambiguously refers to religious violence as part of their case against Christianity, they are ignoring this principle. It can happen subtly and is not always easily recognized, but we need to develop our skills in catching it. Our reply should be something like this: "It's true that Christians and religious people have stirred up wars and violence, but do you think that if people truly followed the teachings of Jesus, they would be led to commit acts of violence? If so, which one of Jesus' teachings are you thinking of?"

We could even ask whether we ourselves sometimes act in ways that do not represent the teachings of Jesus well. Of course, we are all guilty of this at some level and we might as well admit it. This principle doesn't only require us to ask skeptics to distinguish Christianity from its abuses; it also calls us to make a distinction between some of our own actions and the teachings of Jesus. Even then, we are called to defend one but not the other.

5. CLARIFY THE SKEPTIC'S OBJECTIONS

I was talking with a Canadian university student from the Middle East one day when he stated that his objection to Christianity was, and I quote, "the Trinity." I immediately asked him what, precisely, his problem with the Trinity was to give him an opportunity to explain. I knew there could be a variety of responses here. This student, after giving the matter some thought, clarified that he believed this doctrine involved a contradiction. I then asked him to point out exactly where the contradiction was. After some effort he hesitantly said, "Well doesn't it teach that there are three Gods and one God at the same time?" With that I knew exactly what I needed to talk about if I was to be helpful to this sincere inquirer. We proceeded to have a fifteen-minute conversation about what precisely constitutes a contradiction, and also what the Christian doctrine of the Trinity does and does not teach.

My main reply to this young student was that while this doctrine surely involves mystery, it would be difficult for anyone to show a contradiction in it. If this doctrine taught that God existed as three persons and also one person at the same time, it would be contradictory, but that is not what it teaches. Or on the other hand, if it taught that there were three Gods and also one God at the same time, then that, too, would be contradictory but, again, that is not what it teaches. In a nutshell, this doctrine teaches that on the divine level more than one person can be combined together in one being. Theologians speak of one substance and three persons. We can't really imagine it because on our level, one person is always one being but, as C. S. Lewis shows with an illustration of the cube having six sides but still being one cube, we can get some faint notion of it. I directed this student to his explanation of this teaching for his own further reflection.[5]

Mystery, I said, was something I did not find surprising. After all, would we really expect descriptions of an infinite God to be clear and simple all the way through?

In fact, as C. S. Lewis notes, this concept is certainly not something any of us could have guessed. Rather than being a difficulty, however, this is one of the reasons he became a Christian. Reality itself, he observed, is usually not the sort of thing we would have guessed, once we understand it. If Christianity presented the kind of teachings about God we would have expected, Lewis would have felt we were simply making them up. The doctrine of the Trinity, most certainly, does not look like a teaching anyone would have made up.

> Objections often come in hazy, imprecise forms, and clarifying before proceeding further allows us to focus our discussion on the most important questions.

But notice the point here. This all came about through following one rather simple principle: clarify and pinpoint the person's objection. I have found this one principle astonishingly helpful in my own discussions with people. Objections often come in hazy, imprecise forms, and clarifying before proceeding further allows us to focus our discussion on the most important questions.

This principle is helpful in conversations with any kind of skeptic, but it is especially helpful for the new kind of skeptic. This type of skeptic understands the typical responses Christians are likely to give and will usually formulate challenges in such a way that those replies will seem inadequate. Before attempting to respond to the question, it is critical to press this person to clarify precisely what his or her objection is.

On a different occasion, I was in conversation with another young man who had grown up a Christian but had turned away and was now a passionate atheist. When I asked him what reasons he would give for thinking atheism was true, his reply surprised me. It was not up to him, he said, to give reasons for his atheism. The burden of proof is on the positive, not the negative. Atheists are merely making the negative claim that there is no God. Theists, on the other hand, are making the positive claim that there is a God and, therefore, it is up to them to provide reasons for their claim.

It didn't take me long to realize that if we accept this framework for the discussion, then the job of supporting atheism has just become far easier. It means that while one who believes in God must bring reasons for thinking God exists and have them evaluated, the atheist merely has to listen to these arguments, find them unconvincing for any number of reasons, and then return to the default position, which is atheism. I also knew that, when viewing them in isolation, finding philosophical arguments for virtually any position to be unconvincing is a fairly simple task. It's a far different matter when one needs to compare arguments for competing positions to see which ones are stronger. But all that was swept aside when my friend claimed that the burden of proof is on the person making the positive claim, never on the person making a negative claim.

How does one respond to such a sweeping claim? In keeping with the principle of clarifying the skeptic's objections, I decided to zero in on his statement and ask him to clarify it further. I asked him if he was truly willing to stand by the statement that the burden of proof is *always* on the person making a positive claim. I emphasized the word *always* because I thought he might wish to qualify it. He answered with an emphatic yes. I then gave an example of a negative claim: the Holocaust did not happen. "Is it really true," I pressed, "that the person making that statement has no burden of proof to support it, that the burden of proof is always and only on the person claiming that the Holocaust did happen?"

He thought for a minute and then began revising his claim. In time, he admitted that if a person said they believed the Holocaust did not happen, they would indeed have a burden of proof to support it. In other words, this negative claim did carry with it a burden of proof. I then asked him if this also applied to a person who said they believed God did not exist. After some time, he agreed to this as well. I do not want to leave the impression that this ended the discussion, but it did lead to a more fruitful one and even to others with other people since then. And it all started with clarifying his objection.

I have found the following five clarifying questions helpful in my own conversations:

- "What exactly do you mean with that statement/question?" This is particularly helpful when a statement or question could be understood in more than one way, as many can.

- "Are you willing to apply your statement consistently?" This was the question I used in my discussion above with the skeptic who argued that the burden of proof is always on the person making the positive claim.

- "How does your objection disprove Christianity? Exactly which teaching or tenet of Christianity is shown to be false by what you say?" This is helpful when a person has claimed their objection justifies their rejection of Christianity, that it disproves it.

- "Which arguments are you thinking of?" This is a relevant question when a person has stated that the arguments for key Christian truth claims, such as the existence of God, the reliability of the Bible, the resurrection or even existence of Jesus, and so on, are all invalid or unconvincing.

- "Have you read any articles from credible Christian sources that support the Christian teaching that you reject? If not, how do you know the arguments for this position are weaker than the ones against it?" I have found these two questions helpful when a person claims she has read certain arguments against a particular Christian teaching and now has reasons for rejecting it.

Perhaps you can think of other helpful clarifying questions. If you can, I encourage you to use them, both for your sake and for the person with whom you are talking.

6. TAKE HEART IN THE RESOURCES AVAILABLE TO YOU

Let's return to my friend Steve. You'll remember that his skeptical colleague had been raised in the church and had studied the Bible more than many Christians. After finding problems he couldn't solve, he compiled a list of objections to Christianity. Over time, it became long and included challenges Steve had not heard before.

If we are willing to engage others with the message of Christianity, as Steve was, we too just might face a new kind of skeptic like Steve's colleague, with objections to our faith that seem so hard and so new to us that we begin to doubt that good answers for them even exist. We may think, "Where can I go for help? I'll bet none of my friends, or my church, or my pastor have ever heard these ones before." Thoughts like these have the potential to throw our faith into a tailspin.

While there are a number of things we can do in response, the first thing we should remind ourselves of is that even the toughest and newest-seeming objections you or I face have already been made by someone somewhere, present or past. Furthermore, someone, or more likely more than one person, has probably responded to them as well. No objection that you or I ever hear is absolutely new and has not been answered in some way. The resources at our disposal are enormous and should be a source of great encouragement to us.

> Even the toughest and newest-seeming objections you or I face have already been made by someone somewhere, present or past.

The reality is that no one Christian will have thoughtful answers to every single challenge that a skeptic could aim at Christianity. That's just unrealistic. But that is the beauty of the Christian community; it is large, rich, and deep, and it contains many scholars and thinkers who have wrestled with a huge number of issues and challenges to Christian teachings. Somewhere in the Christian community there will, undoubtedly, be thoughtful discussions of the challenges you hear. It is your task to find them and determine whether they are suitable answers to a skeptic or your own doubts.

None of us are alone in this, and none of us needs to be discouraged in the face of new or hard challenges. There is always help available somewhere regardless of the issue someone raises, whether it concerns the evil and suffering in the world, alleged contradictions in the Bible, so-called religious violence, the supposed impossibility of miracles, differences in the texts upon which our Bible is based, the emergence of new gospels, questions of how our Bible was formed, changes in official church teaching over time, or any other issue.

It's just a matter of digging or asking around and perhaps acquiring a few good resources of our own. We are in the happy position of being able to make use of the work done by others who have traveled this way before.

7. USE HUMOR AND ENJOY THE PROCESS

You may think I'm just looking for a light-hearted way to end this chapter, but actually I want to point out that the task of drawing people to God is God's work. This fact underlies everything we do when we respond to challenges to Christian faith.

This is what Paul says in his second letter to the Corinthians. In this letter, he teaches the radical idea that the gospel message we bring to the world is actually veiled to people who do not believe it. He goes as far as to say that they cannot understand it. In other words, the very people who need to hear it cannot get it. Their spiritual eyes are closed unless God makes his light shine in their hearts and enables them to understand it (2 Corinthians 4:3–6).

As I considered the impact of this idea, I realized that when we are involved in the task of responding to skeptics (whether they once believed or not), we are actually involved in God's work. He could do it just fine without our assistance, but he has chosen to allow us to be a part of what he is doing in the world. But it also means that we can take all the pressure off ourselves for drawing any person, however challenging, to Christ. That's not something we could ever do. It is God's work. Our privilege is to represent the greatest message in the world and leave the results in the hands of God. There is true joy in that, and we should enjoy ourselves as we

> Our privilege is to represent the greatest message in the world and leave the results in the hands of God.

do it. Not only can it motivate us to prepare well, but it can enable us to rest easy as we carry out this privilege with those around us.

Furthermore, it's worth remembering that looking like we've just been sucking on lemons does not increase our effectiveness. Just ask yourself how drawn you would be to someone who is trying to persuade or sell you something if they seemed pessimistic and unhappy. The seriousness of our work does not mean it has to be performed with a sour outlook on life. In fact, if anything, the opposite is true. William Wilberforce, the British parliamentarian who spent thirty years fighting such horrible evils as slavery, child labor, and harsh debtor laws, was also known as the funniest member of the British Parliament. It was said that people sitting near him were often brought to tears laughing at the comments he would mumble under his breath during the speeches of others.

The happier and friendlier we are, the more fun and enjoyment we seem to be getting out of engaging others with the gospel, the more effective we are bound to be. And why not? The pressure is off because we remember whose work it really is to speak to the challenges of a new kind of skeptic.

Part 2

Answering Objections

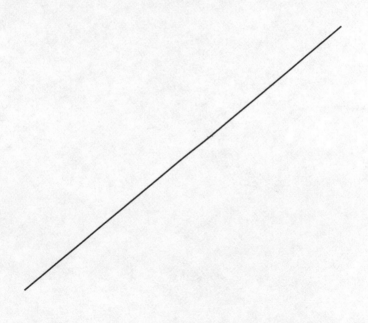

3. Why Is the Old Testament God So Violent?

BARTON PRIEBE

A few years ago, I reconnected with an old friend through Facebook. Since he had once professed to be a Christian, I was surprised to see that he now listed his religious belief as "apostate." We met for coffee and quickly began speaking of the journey that led him to reject Christianity. The first issue he raised was his problems with the Bible, and specifically what he perceived to be the immoral character of God in commanding the use of violence against the Canaanites. Deuteronomy 20:16–18 provides a succinct summary of God's directives:

> In the cities of the nations the LORD your God is giving you as an inheritance, do not leave alive anything that breathes. Completely destroy them—the

Hittites, Amorites, Canaanites, Perizzites, Hivites
and Jebusites—as the LORD your God has commanded you. Otherwise, they will teach you to
follow all the detestable things they do in worshiping their gods, and you will sin against the LORD
your God.

The book of Joshua goes on to describe how Israel, at the
command of God, invaded and conquered the Canaanites.
This, my friend went on to say, is genocide, and proves
God is an unjust moral monster who should be utterly
rejected.

This objection to the God of the Bible is nothing new.
One recent example of it is prominent scientist and atheist Richard Dawkins's reference to the war on Canaan as
"ethnic cleansing" in his book *The God Delusion*. He says:

The Bible story of Joshua's destruction of Jericho,
and the invasion of the Promised Land in general,
is morally indistinguishable from Hitler's invasion
of Poland, or Saddam Hussein's massacres of the
Kurds and the Marsh Arabs. ... Do not think, by
the way, the God character in the story nurses any

doubts or scruples about the massacres and geno-
cides that accompanied the seizing of the Promised
Land.[1]

In light of this, Dawkins accuses God of being an "evil
monster"[2] and minces no words in expressing his assessment of God's character:

> The God of the Old Testament is arguably the most
> unpleasant character in all fiction: jealous and
> proud of it; a petty, unjust, unforgiving control-freak;
> a vindictive, *bloodthirsty ethnic cleanser*; a misogy-
> nistic, homophobic, racist, infanticidal, *genocidal*,
> filicidal, pestilential, megalomaniacal, sadomasoch-
> istic, capriciously malevolent bully.[3]

Another well-known atheist, the late journalist
Christopher Hitchens, said that the Canaanites were "pit-
ilessly driven out of their homes to make room for the
ungrateful and mutinous children of Israel," and asserts
that the Bible "contain[s] a warrant for ethnic cleansing ...
and for indiscriminate massacre."[4]

Since God's violence in the Old Testament is one of
the major reasons people reject Christianity, this chapter

will equip you to respond to this issue by looking at the most well-known example, which is the destruction of the Canaanites. We will take a fresh look at this story to discover why God issued his command, uncover the historical facts of what actually happened, and ultimately see what this ancient story has to do with us today. I will end the chapter with a few practical tips for navigating this issue as you engage in everyday conversations with those who, like my friend, reject Christianity because they view God as an evil monster.

> Since God's violence in the Old Testament is one of the major reasons people reject Christianity, this chapter will equip you to respond to this issue by looking at the most well-known example, which is the destruction of the Canaanites.

WHY DID GOD ORDER THE DESTRUCTION OF THE CANAANITES?

Have you ever started watching a movie when it is almost over? It is a very frustrating experience. Why did the angry man shoot the other guy who seemed to be so nice? If you are watching the movie on television, you likely changed the channel. If you walk into the room while others are watching, you will probably just go to another room until it is over. The problem, of course, is that you don't know the whole story. If you had seen the movie from the beginning, it would have made perfect sense. You would have known, for example, that the angry man was an undercover police officer and the "nice" man had abducted a child.

Knowing the whole story changes everything, and so it is with the question of the violence of God. The Bible gives its own backstory for why God ordered the destruction of the Canaanites, but it is given much earlier. The Bible's story begins in Genesis, chapters 1–3, with the declaration that God created everything that exists but that human beings rebelled against their Creator. Genesis 4–11 chronicle the terrible effects on what life is like when humanity turns its collective back on God. People are filled with things like murder, arrogance, revenge, violence, and incest. But the story takes a radical shift in Genesis 12 when God reveals himself to a man named Abram (later to be called "Abraham"). God promises Abram that his descendants will become a great

> Knowing the whole story changes everything, and so it is with the question of the violence of God.

nation, through whom God further promises to bless "all peoples on earth" (Genesis 12:3). This grand plan of blessing is elaborated in Genesis 15 when God promises to give Abram's descendants the very land on which he is standing—the land of Canaan: "I am the LORD, who brought you out of Ur of the Chaldeans to give you this land to take possession of it" (Genesis 15:7).

God tells Abram how this will take place and, more importantly for the purposes of this chapter, *when* it will take place: "Then the LORD said to him, 'Know for certain that for *four hundred years* your descendants will be strangers in a country not their own and that they will be enslaved and mistreated there. But I will punish the nation they serve as slaves, and afterward they will come out with great possessions'" (Genesis 15:13–14, emphasis added).

Note three things about the story so far: (1) God promises to make Abraham's descendants into a great nation (later to be called "Israel"); (2) God will give the land of Canaan to Israel; (3) this will not happen until the Israelites have spent four hundred years as slaves in Egypt. In fact, it would be much longer than that. Abraham's wife, Sarah, still had to give birth to his son Isaac, who in turn grew up and fathered Jacob. Jacob eventually had twelve sons who then moved to Egypt. They multiplied in number and became the nation of Israel. It was not until *after* this time span that Israel was enslaved for four hundred years in Egypt. This means God did not actually give Israel the land of Canaan for *well over four hundred years* after he promised it to Abram. The critical question is this: Why wouldn't God give Israel the land of Canaan earlier? Why wait such an incredibly long time?

The Bible gives its own answer just a couple of verses later. Speaking to Abram about the Amorites (the major people group in the land of Canaan during Abram's day), God says, "In the fourth generation your descendants will come back here, *for the sin of the Amorites has not yet reached its full measure*" (Genesis 15:16b, emphasis added). With this pronouncement we discover that the conquest of Canaan is to be understood within the patience and justice of God. How so?

First, God is extremely patient in that he does not bring the sword down on the Amorites for just one sin, or even for one hundred years of sin. God waits and waits for the nations in Canaan to turn away from their sin. Second, God is just. In our society, we work patiently with criminals to rehabilitate them. If they continually break the laws, however, we eventually bring strict justice on them. In like manner, the Bible shows that God waits hundreds of years for the Canaanites to turn away from their sins, which included idolatry, child sacrifice, bestiality, incest, temple prostitution, and violence.[5] But eventually, those sins cross a moral threshold and, like any just judge, God punishes them.

If this is an act of divine justice, then it would be inaccurate to call it "genocide," as Dawkins and my friend have. Genocide is fueled by racial hatred, but the Bible never asserts, or even hints, that the Canaanites were destroyed because of their ethnicity. God did not order the destruction of the Canaanites because of their race; he destroyed them because of their sin. This is not, therefore, a case of genocide or ethnic cleansing; it is a case of capital punishment.

The Bible's explanation of the violence of God against the Canaanites can be summarized as follows: The conquest of Canaan was not instigated by a bloodthirsty tribal deity but was commanded by God to execute justice against a specific people living in a specific time whose wickedness had reached a tipping point. Deuteronomy 9:5 echoes this assertion when God says to Israel, "It is not because of your righteousness or your integrity that you are going in to take possession of their land; but on account of the wickedness of these nations, the LORD your God will drive them out before you, to accomplish what he swore to your fathers, to Abraham, Isaac and Jacob" (compare Deuteronomy 20:16–18).

But why use violence at all? Is it ever justified?

JUST AND UNJUST USES OF VIOLENCE

On October 22, 2014, Michael Zehaf-Bibeau walked onto Parliament Hill, the center of Canada's government. He fatally shot Corporal Nathan Cirillo, who was standing guard at the Canadian National War Memorial. He then entered the Parliament building where members of the Parliament of Canada, including the Prime Minister, were meeting. A shootout began, and the Commons Sergeant at Arms, Kevin Vickers, shot and killed Zehaf-Bibeau.

In this example, we see two types of violence. One of them the vast majority of us do not accept as morally just. The other we are more likely to accept as just, even if we believe it is always undesirable to take someone's life. We do not accept Zehaf-Bibeau's using violence to shoot Corporal Cirillo in cold blood. However, most people accept Kevin Vickers's using violence to kill Zehaf-Bibeau. This does not mean that we think the violence Kevin Vickers used is nice or pleasant, but it does mean that most accept it as a necessary and just act.

Likewise, each Remembrance Day (for Canadians) or Veterans' Day (for Americans) we are reminded of the violence of previous wars our countries fought in. As we recall these wars, we make a distinction between just and unjust uses of violence. In remembering World War II, for example, we *do not* accept the violence of the Nazis in systematically murdering six million Jews. Yet most people *do* accept the violence of the Allied nations in defeating Hitler's forces.

In a similar way, the Bible's answer does not make the destruction of the Canaanites any less violent, but it does frame the violence in a different category.

WHAT ACTUALLY HAPPENED
IN CANAAN?

After forty years of wandering in the wilderness, Israel's military was vast in number, armed to the teeth, and ready to fight. The Canaanites, lulled into a false sense of security by their idyllic paradise "flowing with milk and honey" (Exodus 33:3), were caught by surprise. In a blitz-krieg of shock and awe, the Israelites used their superior power to crush the peaceful but naïve Canaanites. Israel's onslaught must have been a spectacular display of force as city after city was overpowered and the Canaanite population exterminated.

This is the story skeptics like Dawkins, Hitchens, and my friend imagine in their minds. The only problem is that such a story is precisely that—imagination. History paints a very different picture. There are four factors that, properly understood, should cause us to think very differently about what actually happened in Canaan.[6]

First, Israel was a nation of slaves who dared to go up against a violently oppressive empire, not an army routing a peace-loving Canaanite people. Israel had just come out of four hundred years of slavery and had been wandering in the wilderness for forty years. This ragtag group of ex-slaves was up against a world superpower that had engulfed and destroyed other nations. Israel was outgunned and outmanned, for Canaan had heavily fortified military outposts (such as Jericho) as well as the most advanced weaponry of their day. Joshua Ryan Butler writes,

> You expect the grade-school bully to take on the weakling with lunch money; you don't expect him to take on the high school wrestling team. You expect a pirate to capture a vessel lost at sea; you don't expect him to declare open war on the Spanish Armada. You expect a Third World dictator to abuse scattered dissenters; you don't expect him to hop in his personal jet and take on the US Air Force. ... Israel is a nation of fearful, intimidated slaves facing off with the mightiest imperial powerhouses of the ancient world.[7]

Second, Israel attacked military strongholds, not concentrated civilian populations. In the ancient Middle East, most people lived in the countryside. The cities of Canaan (such as Jericho and Ai) were not like modern cities where people gather to live and do business. Rather, cities were military outposts used to guard the civilian populations living beyond them, much like the Great Wall of China was built to protect the people on the inside of the wall. Jericho, for example, was positioned at the junction of three roads leading to the cities of Jerusalem, Bethel, and Ophrah, and thus protected the Jordan Valley and the hill country to the west. Israel's violence, therefore, was directed toward the military installments—against the combatants and their kings stationed there.* Paul Copan writes, "All the archeological evidence indicates that no civilian populations existed at Jericho, Ai, and other cities mentioned in Joshua. ... Jericho was a small settlement of probably one hundred or fewer soldiers. This is why all of Israel could circle it seven times and then do battle against it on the same day."[8]

Third, we often find it troubling that the Bible speaks of Israel's victory in all-encompassing terms: "So Joshua subdued the whole region. ... He left no survivors. He totally destroyed all who breathed" (Joshua 10:40). Yet

---

* The references to "kings" also demonstrate this. The kings of Canaanite military bases like Jericho were not kings in the sense we use today. They were military leaders subordinate to higher officials who lived elsewhere.

Joshua himself acknowledges elsewhere that this is not literally the case. Is he lying? No, he is simply using the accepted rhetoric of his day.

This way of talking is similar to the language the sporting world uses today. If our hockey team beats their rivals 7–2, we say, "We killed them! They couldn't do anything against us! We totally destroyed them!" If such talk is taken literally, it sounds as if the other team hardly got a shot on goal, let alone put two pucks behind our goaltender. Taken literally, such grandiose language makes it sound like our team won 19–0, but we all understand the context. No one is lying or seeking to deceive; it is simply an accepted, figurative way of speaking—hyperbole.

In like manner, the accepted warfare rhetoric of the time included a fair amount of hyperbole. For instance, the Egyptian Pharaoh Thutmose III (fifteenth century BC) bragged, "The numerous army of Mitanni was overthrown within the hour, annihilated totally, like those (now) not existent." In reality, Mitanni's armies were not totally destroyed; they fought throughout the fifteenth and fourteenth centuries BC.[9]

The same type of hyperbolic language appears in Joshua. For example, Joshua 11:21 states, "At that time Joshua went and destroyed the Anakites from the hill country: from Hebron, Debir and Anab, from all the hill country of Judah, and from all the hill country of Israel. Joshua totally destroyed them and their towns. No Anakites were left in Israelite territory." Yet only three chapters later, this very same Joshua gives Caleb permission to drive out the Anakites in the "hill country" who possess "cities" that are "large and fortified" (Joshua 14:12–14).

Although the book of Joshua speaks in terms of total destruction, the end of the book assumes the continued existence of the Canaanites, because Joshua warns the Israelites about following their destructive ways (see Joshua 23:7, 12–13; compare 15:63; 16:10; 17:13; Judges 2:10–13). Likewise, Deuteronomy 7:2 commands Israel to "defeat" and "utterly destroy" the Canaanites and yet goes on in verses 3–5 to command them not to intermarry or make treaties with the Canaanites they "destroy." Copan summarizes the point:

A closer look at the biblical text reveals a lot more nuance—and a lot less bloodshed. In short, the conquest of Canaan was far less widespread and harsh than many people assume. Like his ancient Near Eastern contemporaries, Joshua used the language of conventional warfare rhetoric. ... He was speaking the language that everyone in his day would have understood. ... The language is typically exaggerated and full of bravado, depicting total devastation. The knowing ancient Near Eastern reader recognized this as hyperbole; the accounts weren't understood to be literally true. ... Joshua was just saying he had fairly well trounced the enemy.[10]

Finally, Israel's conquest of Canaan is described more in terms of "driving out" than of "killing off." To drive out means to expel or eject, which assumes the people were alive—not dead. God, like a landlord whose patience with his unruly tenants has run out, was kicking out the Canaanites. The references to driving out/dispossessing are, in fact, more numerous than the references to destroying (see, for example, Exodus 23:30; Deuteronomy 11:23; Joshua 23:9).[11]

WHAT KIND OF GOD
DO YOU WANT?

Despite all that has been said so far, many will simply say, "I just can't believe in a God who would do this." But what would they have wanted God to do? Consider how we would react if God had *not* acted to put a stop to the horrific evil and violence. When evil happens in the world, people often shake their fist at God and say, "How can I believe in you when you allow evil in the world? Why don't you stop those who rape women, enslave children, behead journalists, or shoot Canadian soldiers on Parliament Hill?" In other words, such people are saying, "I can't believe in a God who *doesn't* put a stop to evil. I want a God who is just!" Most of us probably share this sentiment. However, when it comes to a case such as the Canaanites, in which God did stop their evil practices, we say, in essence, "I can't believe in a God who *does* put a stop to evil. What God did to the Canaanites was not fair. Why was God so harsh in punishing them?"

> The question we must all face is, do we want a God who stops evil or don't we? We can't have it both ways.

The question we must all face is, Do we want a God who stops evil or don't we? We can't have it both ways. We can't say, "God, we won't worship you because you *don't* punish evil," and then say, "God, we won't worship you because you *do* punish evil."[12]

Still, many will say, "I cannot accept all this talk of God's wrath and punishment. I believe in a God of love and tolerance, not a God of anger and judgment." But is a non-wrathful, non-judgmental God truly a loving God? Miroslav Volf, the Yale theologian who lived through the nightmare of ethnic strife in the former Yugoslavia, writes the following:

> I used to think that wrath was unworthy of God. Isn't God love? Shouldn't divine love be beyond wrath? God is love, and God loves every person and every creature. That's exactly why God is wrathful against some of them. My last resistance to the idea of God's wrath was a casualty of the war in the former Yugoslavia, the region from which I come. According to some estimates, 200,000 people were killed and over 3,000,000 were displaced. *My* villages and cities were destroyed, *my* people shelled day in and day out, some of them brutalized beyond imagination, and I could not imagine God not being angry. ... How did God react to the carnage?

By doting on the perpetrators in a grandfatherly fashion? By refusing to condemn the bloodbath but instead affirming the perpetrators' basic goodness? Wasn't God fiercely angry with them? Though I used to complain about the indecency of the idea of God's wrath, I came to think that I would have to rebel against a God who *wasn't* wrathful at the sight of the world's evil. God isn't wrathful in spite of being love. God is wrathful *because* God is love.[13]

The God of the Bible, therefore, is shown to be extremely patient and yet also a God who cares about good and evil. His commitment to justice means that he will not allow something like the slaughter of babies through child sacrifice to go on indefinitely but will eventually bring justice on those who commit such atrocities.

WHAT THE CANAANITES HAVE TO DO WITH US

To return to my earlier analogy, just as you cannot reject a movie as being absurd when you only started watching it in the middle (and thus need to understand the backstory), so also you cannot judge a movie's true worth if you turn it off before the big plot twist occurs near the end. What would *The Lord of the Rings* be without the final scene of the ring falling into the fires of Mount Doom? Imagine someone turning off the movie just before this critical scene because they felt the story was too dark and depressing.

I've just said that those who accuse God of being unjust for ordering the violent destruction of the Canaanites often do not interact with the backstory of God's patience and his justice, as well as the sin of the Canaanites, which brought about their judgment. But likewise, neither do they follow the story through to the end of the Bible. When we place the judgment of the Canaanites within this larger story, we suddenly find (to our intense discomfort and distaste) that this ancient episode has direct relevance to us. The Bible teaches that the judgments of God (like Noah's flood, the destruction of Sodom and Gomorrah, and, indeed, the driving out of the Canaanites) are previews of a future day of judgment that God will bring on the whole world. In this sense, the Canaanites are a representative picture of all humanity, both ancient and modern, living in rebellion against God.

There are few things more offensive to people today than the idea that we are guilty of wrongdoing and will someday be judged. Surely we do not deserve God's punishment. After all, the argument goes, we are not bad people.

Or are we? Like the Canaanites, have we not turned away from our Creator who gives us life and breath and everything else, in order to follow our own desires and be our own gods? Like the Canaanites, are we not a culture that rejects God's rules on sexuality as we experiment with and pursue every conceivable type of sexual gratification? Like the Canaanites, do we not enjoy entertainment that glorifies extreme violence, horror, murder, and bloodshed? Like the Canaanites, do we not sacrifice our children? It may not be part of a worship ritual, but do we not sacrifice our unborn children by the millions to the gods of career, a woman's choice, our own convenience, or a gender bias that values boys more than girls?

> We all want a God who is just, but it is precisely the justice of God that is our great problem.

We all want a God who is just, but it is precisely the justice of God that is our great problem. After all, if we are guilty of wrongdoing, it means we, like the Canaanites, will eventually face judgment. Who can stand before such a just God?

THE TWIST IN THE PLOT

It is right here, at the point when the Bible's message is most dark, that the big twist in the plot occurs. The message of the Bible is that, despite our wrongdoing, God's heart is for, not against, his creation. The entire story of the Bible is the story of how God has worked out a way to rescue people from his own wrath. God promised Abraham, "All peoples on earth will be blessed through you" (Genesis 12:3). God has prepared a way to be just *and* to forgive us for our wrongdoing, which means we can escape the punishment we deserve.

This solution to the punishment and violence of God begins with a plan God made before he created the world. In eternity past, God planned to enter into the world in order that he might take the punishment we deserve upon himself. This is why the Bible says Jesus "was chosen before the creation of the world," and that he is "the Lamb that was slain from the creation of the world" (1 Peter 1:20; Revelation 13:8).

We must not, however, think that Jesus was forced to follow God the Father's plan that led to his violent death. Jesus repeatedly stated that when he laid down his life it would be done willingly: "No one takes [my life] from me, but I lay it down of my own accord. I have authority to lay it down and authority to take it up again" (John 10:18). In other words, the Son voluntarily accepted the mission assigned to him by his Father. On the cross, Jesus, the one man in history who did not deserve judgment, took on himself the punishment we deserved, that we might have peace with God: "He was pierced for our transgressions, he was crushed for our iniquities; the punishment that brought us peace was on him, and by his wounds we are healed" (Isaiah 53:5).

In pioneer days, families would sometimes find themselves about to be burned alive by a prairie fire. They might walk out of their house and see a great plume of black smoke in the distance. They knew the wind was whipping up a fire and pushing it toward their homestead. Prairie fires burn hot and fast, reaching seven hundred degrees Fahrenheit, traveling at speeds of up to six hundred feet per minute. There was only one hope for families in such a situation: they would run into their fields and set their own crops on fire. As their crops were consumed, a large patch of burned ground would form and the entire family would stand in the middle of it. The fire would race toward them but would suddenly stop at the edge of the burned ground. The fire would turn aside to the left and the right, but it would not engulf the family because the ground on which they stood had already been burned.

The Bible presents Jesus Christ as the burned patch of ground for sinners. Since Jesus voluntarily took the wrath that is due to sinners on himself, those who stand in him will escape the future judgment of God, for "[Jesus] rescues us from the coming wrath" (1 Thessalonians 1:10). It is because Jesus is this safe patch of burned ground that the Bible calls people to entrust themselves to him: "Whoever believes in the Son has eternal life, but whoever rejects the Son will not see life, for God's wrath remains on him" (John 3:36).

The grand story of the Bible is a celebration of what God has done to rescue sinners through the violent death of Jesus Christ. Over and over, the biblical writers revel in and exult over this good news: "Since we have now been justified by his blood, how much more shall we be saved from God's wrath through him," and "There is now no condemnation for those who are in Christ Jesus" (Romans 5:9; 8:1). The Bible's story is not about God seeking to destroy humanity. Rather, it is the story of how God, in grace and love, has found a way to be just and to forgive people. Out of love, the Father sent his Son

> The Bible's story is not about God seeking to destroy humanity. Rather, it is the story of how God, in grace and love, has found a way to be just and to forgive people.

Jesus into this world to bear in himself the punishment that we deserve in order that God's justice might be satisfied and that we might be forgiven and reconciled to God.

TALKING POINTS

While no conversation will follow an exact script, the following talking points will help you have a meaningful conversation on the issue of God and violence, especially with regard to the Israelite conquest of Canaan.

1. *Show agreement:* We all want a God who is just and a world where justice prevails. This desire for justice should be affirmed, for Christians

believe it is a God-given desire that reflects the fact that we are made in the image of God, who is just.

2. *Clear away stumbling blocks:* In order to help people see that the God of the Bible is truly just, we need to clear away the stumbling blocks that make God appear unjust. To do this you can:

   • Question the rhetoric of "genocide" and "ethnic cleansing" and affirm that God hates racism and violence based on race.

   • Stress the importance of reading the Bible's stories within their context, as the context will often explain difficult passages.

   • Give the biblical reason for God's command to drive out and destroy the Canaanites and talk about the patience and justice of God in dealing with cultures that do things like sacrifice babies.

   • Clear up the mental picture that many have in their minds of what happened in Canaan by pointing to the historical facts.

- Talk about just and unjust uses of violence using examples such as genocide versus just war, or terrorism versus a policeman killing a suicide bomber.

3. *Expose inconsistencies:* Point out the problems with saying both "God, we won't worship you because you *do* punish evil" and "God, we won't worship you because you *don't* punish evil." Not punishing evil would make God unjust.

4. *Point to Jesus:* Place the story of the Canaanite conquest within the wider story of the Bible by showing how, in Jesus, God is both just and merciful.

Although my friend did not change his mind that day, I hope this chapter will equip you to show others that the God of the Bible is exactly what we want him to be—a just God who cares about matters of good and evil as well as a gracious God who shows mercy to all who come to him through Jesus Christ.

4. Why Does God Allow Suffering?

CHRIS PRICE

N ot long ago, a friend's wife left him. Leading up to the split their home was flooded with tension, tears, and strife. In the midst of all this, their three-year-old daughter started putting Band-Aids all over her body. She knew she hurt, but she couldn't find the wound—so she put bandages all over in hopes of making the pain go away.

But it didn't. It is heartbreaking to discover at such a young age that there is no bandage for the soul.

I've been a pastor for just over twelve years, and walking with people through some of the darkest seasons of their lives is part of my calling. In a congregation of several hundred people, it seems as if someone is always struggling with chronic pain, relational distress, a cancer

diagnosis, or losing a loved one. And I haven't even mentioned the terrible stuff that people do to one another;
abuse, war, rape, slavery, and oppression are just some
of the horrors that human beings have unleashed on one
another.

The experience of suffering and evil is the most frequently raised objection to the Christian faith by believers and unbelievers alike. There are no easy answers, but
in this chapter I will examine two possible reasons that
may explain why God allows evil and suffering: the value
of human freedom and the refining nature of trials and
difficulties. Then, after a brief interlude, I will explore
ways in which the Bible addresses the problem of evil
and provides hope in the midst of a hurting world—hope
beyond a Band-Aid solution.

THE VALUE OF HUMAN FREEDOM

Growing up, I was occasionally smitten with girls who
didn't give me the time of day. In those moments, it is
tempting to wonder what it would be like if I could mix
together a love potion that would simulate all the feelings
and behaviors normally associated with the experience
of being in love. All it takes is one or two potion-filled

chocolates for the uninterested individual to become infatuated with you.

Though it might feel great for a while, the relationship is a sham, isn't it? The other person doesn't really love you; he or she is being unwillingly and unknowingly subjected to these euphoric feelings by a potion of your own concoction. If the potion isn't administered, the passion won't be reciprocated. The potion has turned them into a puppet on a string; they are one step up from a robot and two steps up from an inflatable doll.

There is no true, genuine, loving relationship without the free choice of both parties involved. Free choice is required for love to exist, and love is central to the meaning and value of our human experience. As Professor Slughorn says to Harry Potter and his classmates, a love potion "doesn't really create love, of course. It is impossible to manufacture or imitate love."[1] Or to quote theologian and pastor Greg Boyd, "Pre-programmed agents would not genuinely *be* loving. Love can only be genuine if it's freely chosen. Which means,

> There is no true, genuine, loving relationship without the free choice of both parties involved.

unless a personal agent has the capacity to choose against love, they don't really have the capacity to choose *for* it."[2]

It is not just love that freedom makes possible. Without freedom of the will, rationality would also be impossible. It is freedom that enables you to truly weigh the pros and cons of an argument, probe the logic, and come to a conclusion about whether you find the attempted answer compelling. Without freedom, your sense that you are evaluating the feasibility of proposals would be illusory.

This might be a startling suggestion, but think about it with me.

If you are not free, your thoughts are determined by factors outside of your control. You only think you are weighing a position and freely following the evidence where it leads, when in reality you are simply dancing to the tune dictated by the neurons firing in your brain, which know neither truth nor reason. We discount people's speech or behavior as irrational the moment we discover they are caused by a tumor growing in their brain. But if we are not free, all thought is like that (the result of non-rational causes unrealized by us). Therefore, all thought would be invalid, including this one. As biologist

J. B. S. Haldane once said, "If my mental processes are determined wholly by the motions of atoms in my brain, I have no reason to suppose my beliefs are true ... and hence I have no reason for supposing my brain to be composed of atoms."[3] It is the ultimate self-defeating position. To reject free will is to embrace some form of determinism, which means, in the words of Christian apologist Abdu Murray, "even as you read these words, the assessments you're making about the value of my arguments aren't rational reactions—they're just *chemical* reactions."[4]

The above argument means that I cannot rationally dismiss the value of freedom without affirming its value at the very same moment. So, rather than energetically sawing off the branch that bears us up, it seems better to admit that freedom is necessary for love *and* for reason.

Freedom is also necessary for virtue and moral development to be attainable. We don't praise or blame people if we discover that they were forced to act in a certain manner. If you perform a kind act with a gun to your head, the action can't be attributed to your good character. You had little choice in the matter. If my solution to my son's bad language were to put duct tape on his mouth, it would make no sense to praise him for not cussing me out. I removed that option from him. This implies that a reasonable degree of freedom is also required for virtue and character development.

Freedom of the will also provides the underlying rationale for holding criminals accountable for their crimes, as well as awarding heroes with statues in the park. Former cold-case detective J. Warner Wallace says, "If determinism is true, our efforts to rightly praise or blame the actions of ourselves or others seems a nonsensical endeavor; our efforts at justice seem equally pointless. Perhaps this is why the Supreme Court has rejected determinism and cited free will as the foundation of our legal system."[5] Apart from a meaningful sense of self-determination, punishing a criminal for a crime would be as irrational as beating your car for breaking down. The car had no choice in the matter, and neither did the accused.

FREEDOM AND
THE PROBLEM OF EVIL

Freedom of the will is central to what makes our human experience so unique. Without it, we wouldn't have love, reason, or morality. But to be free to love is also to be free to hate. To be free to cultivate virtue also allows us to indulge in vice. To be free to reason is also to be free to embrace folly and resist the truth.

Freedom is a double-edged sword.

From the Christian perspective, God created us with free will because he wants us to share in his love, know his truth (reason), and take on the character of his goodness (virtue). C. S. Lewis sums up this logic nicely when

> Freedom is a double-edged sword.

he writes, "Free will is what has made evil possible. Why, then, did God give [us] free will? Because free will, though it makes evil possible, is also the only thing that makes possible any love or goodness or joy worth having. A world ... of creatures that worked like machines would hardly be worth creating."[6]

Sometimes people will acknowledge the value of freedom but object, "Can't God just give us freedom and intervene every time we choose wrongly?" But imagine what this type of world would be like. When I try to hit you with a bat, it turns into a pool noodle. If I try and drown you, you grow gills. When a drunk gets into a car, it turns to Jell-O. The problem with this option is that it describes a cartoon world. There is no genuine freedom here. Virtue becomes a meaningless concept. Even worse, this solution doesn't deal with the wrong, hurtful desires in our hearts. In fact, this world would nurture evil in our hearts because we can act on wrong intentions without any consequences. This is not, all things considered, a better world.

Others object that free will can't explain natural evil—things that have no clear cause rooted in freedom, like tornadoes and diseases. However, some Christians would disagree about the ultimate cause of these things. They would point out that Adam's and Eve's freely chosen rebellion fractured the natural world in unforeseen ways, leading to disease and a lack of protection from what we label as natural disasters. Other Christians would point to the freedom exercised by angelic beings in rebellion against God causing sickness and other types of ills that indicate a world out of sync with its creator.

A third group of Christian philosophers has pointed out that, in order for free will to be enjoyed, there is a need for fixed laws to regulate our shared environment. If these laws could be suspended on a regular and/or erratic basis, life would be chaotic and human interaction would be near impossible. The downside of this regularity and predictability is that it not only allows life to thrive, it can also lead to some instances of natural evil. The same fire that can warm our hands and cook our food can burn us if we get too close. The law of gravity keeps us grounded, but it can also harm us when we are toddlers first learning to walk or drunken college students who have forgotten how to walk. As Dallas Willard says,

> A world with laws of nature ... in which you have the ability to make "good choices" or not with full awareness of the consequences, is the only environment that will give individual human beings the opportunity to develop a personality and character of their own—whether to their glory or detriment. If you are going to have moral agents in community, you must have something very like our world.[7]

Now, whatever one thinks about the attempt to tie natural evil to the misuse of human freedom, it should be clear that freedom is a precious gift. Without a reasonable degree of self-determination, our lives would lack meaning, and everything that makes our human experience authentically human would be severely diminished if not completely eradicated. But freedom can be abused, and we, as a race, have chosen to do so, and end up reaping the disastrous consequences.[8]

> Without a reasonable degree of self-determination, our lives would lack meaning, and everything that makes our human experience authentically human would be severely diminished if not completely eradicated.

In this way, the value of freedom may explain why God would *allow* moral evil, and, perhaps, even touch on the existence of natural evil. But this type of response is not convincing for all, and it is not an answer that the Bible itself explicitly gives. In light of this shortcoming, what more can be said from a Christian perspective?

GOD WORKS THROUGH SUFFERING

In addition to the value of free will, some Christian thinkers have developed a response to the problem of evil called the soul-making theodicy (a theodicy is an attempt to defend God's goodness in view of the existence of evil). It should be seen as a complementary explanation to the free-will defense laid out above.

Whereas the free-will defense exists to explain why God allowed moral evil, the soul-making theodicy attempts to explain God's purpose in allowing some evil and hardship that results from environmental factors that seem incongruent with the comfort and carefree happiness of people. John Hick, one of the foremost proponents of this view, wrote that "in a world devoid both of dangers to be avoided and rewards to be won, we may assume that virtually no development of the human intellect and imagination would have taken place, and hence no development of the sciences, the arts, human civilization, or culture."[9] In other words, in the soul-making theodicy, the justification for hardship and suffering is the value they produce.

Think of it this way: Have you ever had the opportunity to look after a child that you might consider spoiled—a child not just spoiled by material possessions, but one who is never disciplined or denied anything he or she pleases? I know this seems kind of harsh, but the truth is that spoiled children are more likely to turn out badly because they grow into little tyrants, "me" monsters who demand that life revolve around them. They were brought up to believe the world exists to meet their whims, and if they complain loudly enough, they will get what they want. This breeds entitlement and ruins character.

From childhood onward, human experience seems to teach us that a certain amount of deprivation, of not getting what we want and working through the disappointment, helps form our character. It turns us into the types of people who realize that life is about more than just meeting our needs, and that the world doesn't owe us a whole lot for just showing up. As we grow up and reach adulthood, some hardship may also produce a context in which character and virtue can flourish. The New Testament book of James goes as far as saying, "Consider it pure joy, my brothers and sisters, whenever you face trials of many kinds, because you know that the testing of your faith develops perseverance. Let perseverance finish its work so that you may be mature and complete, not lacking anything" (1:2–4).[10]

> Human experience seems to teach us that a certain amount of deprivation, of not getting what we want and working through the disappointment, helps form our character.

According to James, trials are a part of the maturing process. Difficulties can refine our character in surprising ways that allow us to discover new and meaningful insights about what is valuable in life, leading to new depths of wisdom and maturity. Willard writes,

One does not develop courage without facing danger, patience without trials, wisdom without heart- and brain-racking puzzles, endurance without suffering, or temperance and honesty without temptations. These are the very things we treasure most about people. Ask yourself if you would be willing to be devoid of all these virtues. If your answer is no, then don't scorn the means of obtaining them.[11]

I recently talked to a mother and daughter who lost their husband and father after a two-year battle with cancer. The wife told me that they had both read books about the refining nature of trials and suffering. But now she had witnessed it happen before her very eyes in the life of her husband. She saw that God didn't "waste his sufferings." In response to this, the daughter quietly, and somewhat ruefully, stated, "I prefer the books."

That is an appropriate response to all I have written in this section. I am not trying to make suffering easy or palatable. I also prefer the books to the reality. Even if it's true, I hate it. I may believe it, but I wish it were different. It is true, but I would trade it for another year with my loved ones.

All I'm trying to do in this section is to show that God is big enough to bend it back to his good purposes. God does this in the Bible, and he does it in our own lives.

We see a clear example of this in the story of Joseph in the Old Testament book of Genesis. Joseph suffered painful rejection from his family and was separated from those he loved, moved to Egypt, and was forced to endure a harsh life of slavery. While in Egypt he was unjustly imprisoned, and for thirteen years he faced trials and difficulties until, at the age of thirty, through the miraculous deliverance of God, he was made ruler over Egypt. He was put in the position to save many lives, including the lives of his family and, by extension, God's people. At the end of his life he said to his brothers, "You intended to harm me, but God intended it for good to accomplish what is now being done, the saving of many lives" (Genesis 50:20).

To be clear, to say that God works through suffering is not to explain why God allows every case of unique suffering. It is also true that pain can ruin us as well as refine us, and to a large degree the outcome depends on how we choose to respond. Nevertheless, we can be assured that God doesn't intend to waste our suffering.

God doesn't do evil. We do.

God doesn't turn evil into good either. Evil remains utterly evil. But God can use evil for good, and he can use suffering to accomplish his purposes.

> God doesn't need suffering and evil to accomplish his purposes, but once we introduced it through our sin, God is wise enough and big enough to bend it back toward his good purposes.

God doesn't need suffering and evil to accomplish his purposes, but once we introduced it through our sin, God is wise enough and big enough to bend it back toward his good purposes. The story of Joseph is only one example of this. There are many more.

We just need to remember that while we are in the middle of the pain, we are blinded to the outcome. Languishing in prison, Joseph didn't know he would one day be a prince. We don't see the big picture like God does. We see the tangled threads; God sees the beautiful tapestry, so we often have to trust in the middle what might only make sense at the end. One day, those who trust in Christ will be able to look back over all the heartaches and difficulties in their lives and say, along with Joseph, "That which was intended for evil, God meant for good."

INTERLUDE

Cambodia is a beautiful country with a horrific recent history. A quick Google search will remind you of the killing fields of Pol Pot and the Khmer Rouge. In one particular killing field stands a tree that suffers from a crack in its trunk. It seems like an innocuous crack in an otherwise ordinary tree trunk that has weathered season after season in the Cambodian soil.

But this crack is different. It represents a crack in the moral fabric of the universe—a crack wide enough to swallow the faith of the faithful. The Khmer Rouge smashed thousands of babies' skulls on that tree in the span of several days. The crack is what remains of the massacre, bearing silent witness to the horrors to which humanity can descend.

> We see the tangled threads; God sees the beautiful tapestry, so we often have to trust in the middle what might only make sense at the end.

What answer can you give to explain this atrocity? The answers I've given above—free will or the good that can come from evil—both seem like shallow, trite responses, at least emotionally speaking. Silence and tears seem far more appropriate.

How does one keep faith in a benevolent, powerful God while standing next to a tree like that?

GOD SUFFERS WITH US

Up until now I have explored a few possibilities as to why a good and powerful God might allow evil and suffering. It has not been an exhaustive survey by any means, and there are many other things that could be said. Timothy Keller once wrote, "If you have a God great and transcendent enough to be mad at because he hasn't stopped evil and suffering in the world, then you have (at the same moment) a God great and transcendent enough to have good reasons for allowing it to continue that you can't know. Indeed, you can't have it both ways."[12] I think Keller is right. I don't think it is useful to speculate about the specific reason behind a lot of terrible situations people experience, and I don't want to gloss over the problem that remains. We won't always know why suffering occurs.

In light of that fact, is it still possible to trust God? Is it still reasonable to believe in his power and goodness?

I believe the answer is yes when we consider the person of Jesus.

The answer to the question of whether it is possible to trust God depends on the God we invoke. We need a screaming God, a God in agony, a God hanging on a tree, struggling to breathe, bleeding out on a cruel piece of wood. A forsaken God in what feels to be a God-forsaken world is the paradox at the heart of the Christian tradition. It is the truth standing on its head, legs flaying in the air, begging for prayerful attention. God was, in Christ, reconciling the world to himself. At the point and the place where God seemed most absent, he is present in Christ.

> The answer to the question of whether it is possible to trust God depends on the God we invoke.

Over the question mark of suffering we stamp the cross of Christ. God doesn't just know about suffering. God himself suffered. The late theologian John Stott once wrote:

> [God] laid aside his immunity to pain. He entered our world of flesh and blood, tears and death. He suffered for us. Our sufferings become more manageable in the light of his. There is still a question

mark against human suffering, but over it we boldly stamp another mark, the cross that symbolizes divine suffering. "The cross of Christ ... is God's only self-justification in such a world" as ours.[13]

This is utterly unique to Christianity. The Bible claims that God was in Jesus reconciling the world to himself.

| God didn't have to suffer, but he chooses to in Jesus. | This means that God, in Jesus, experienced rejection, heartache, physical agony, and betrayal. |

He tasted the bitterest parts of human experience. And Jesus did this for one simple reason: he loves you. He loves us.

Nails didn't keep him on the cross. The soldiers didn't keep him on the cross. The mockery of the religious leaders didn't keep him on the cross. Even the mighty Roman Empire didn't keep him on the cross.

Love did.

God didn't have to suffer, but he chooses to in Jesus. Then God raised him from the dead.*

---

* For a defense of the historicity of Jesus' resurrection, see chapter 9, "The Problem of the Resurrection."

The death and resurrection of Jesus informs us that sin and evil are real, which is why Jesus had to die. But it also tells us that the love of God is real, which is why Jesus was willing to die. The good news of Jesus also instructs us that God's power is real, stronger even than the grave, which is why death itself one day will die. Ultimately, the Christian answer to evil is the life, death, and resurrection of Jesus, which allows us to hold the reality of evil and suffering alongside the reality of God's power and love like nothing else does.

This doesn't explain all evil. But it gives us a God we can trust in the middle of it—a God who is with us, so that,

> When human hearts are breaking
>   Under sorrow's iron rod,
> Then they find that self-same aching
>   Deep within the heart of God.[14]

THE FOUR TREES

This chapter has covered a lot of ground, so let me recap the Christian response to the problem of suffering by describing four trees. According to the biblical narrative, the human story began with two trees in a garden. One tree was the tree of life. The other was the tree of the knowledge of good and evil. These two trees created space for the dignity of human decision, a dividing line in the soil that separates us from the lower animals, and a dark possibility of knowledge unhinged from the loving oversight of our Creator. In a sense, the two trees represent a choice, an invitation to trust, an invitation from our Maker to us. These two trees are humanity's welcome into a moral universe that makes meaningful sense of the "ought" and "ought not" of our experience: Freedom. Love. Reason. Morality.

Our rebellion in the garden led to a third tree. This tree grows in Cambodian soil soaked with blood, limbs stretching to the sky in silent protest, testifying to the long slide down from the garden of God to the killing fields of men—a tree of death.

Thankfully, these trees don't get the last word. There is a fourth tree that looms larger than the rest. This tree also represents a choice, but this time the choice is God's. On this tree, instead of humanity thrusting itself into the place of God, God humbly prostrates himself at the feet of his own creation. This is the beginning of the great reversal. This will be the tree where death itself goes to die.

Jesus trod our path, bleeding and broken. He carried this tree on his back, weighed down with our trespasses, limping but still leading us up through the crack in the killing tree, up through the veil into the Father's house, up and up until we reach the fresh air of his new creation. And there he guides us to a river surrounded by a forest glade to discover afresh the hope and beauty of a renewed creation.

> Then I saw "a new heaven and a new earth," for the first heaven and the first earth had passed away. ... "God's dwelling place is now among the people, and he will dwell with them. They will be his people, and God himself will be with them and be their God. 'He will wipe every tear from their eyes. There will be no more death' or mourning or crying or pain, for the old order of things has passed away." He who was seated on the throne said, "I am making everything new!" ... Then the angel showed me the river of the water of life, as clear as crystal, flowing from the throne of God and of the Lamb down the middle of the great street of the city. On each side of the river stood the tree of life, bearing twelve crops of fruit, yielding its fruit

every month. And the leaves of the tree are for the healing of the nations. No longer will there be any curse. (Revelation 21:1, 3–4; 22:1–3)

I sometimes imagine that the tree of life smells of nostalgia, of childhood meanderings through leafy glades run through with gentle glimmers of sunlight searching out the shadows. It is the familiarity of home mixed with the wildness of the woods—the place where you've never been but always belonged. I can almost hear the laughter that joins the gentle chorus of earthy sounds: laughter that promises to spill the secrets of heaven. The divine mirth that rejoiced at the birth of worlds calls to us through the foliage and welcomes us home.

The table is set.

The children have gathered, no longer broken.

The food has been prepared, and there is a place for you.

And there is one more thing I mustn't forget to mention—the tree of life has leaves, and these leaves are unlike any we have ever known, because these leaves are meant for the healing of the nations. The leaves that hid the shame of Adam and Eve will, through Christ, heal ours: No more mourning. No more tears. No more pain. This is our hope.

I remember doing the memorial service of a woman who passed away after an extended battle with cancer. I knew the family well, and I had visited the hospital room near the end of her life to pray with her and the close relatives. When she passed away, her granddaughter, who was in elementary school at the time, drew a picture on a scrap piece of paper and gave it to her mom.

The sketch was of her grandma walking through a doorway into heaven. Right before the doorway was a garbage can, and as her grandma walked past it she threw away her last tissue, because over the doorway into heaven was written, "No more tears." This beautiful young girl handed this picture to her grieving mother, and in the midst of the loss, it provided so much hope and peace.

How do we know this wasn't a false peace or a naïve hope? The answer is the resurrection

> Because Jesus went through death and came out the other side, we can have a real peace and a sure hope.

of Jesus Christ, the center of the Christian faith. Because Jesus went through death and came out the other side, we can have a real peace and a sure hope.

Jesus will make everything new. And his words are trustworthy and true.

CONCLUSION

How do we respond to the problem of evil and suffering, whether faced by ourselves or someone else? I am sure that different readers would like me to emphasize different approaches, but what is likely not at the top of the list is a call to repentance. Yet this is how Jesus himself once responded to individuals who raised the problem of evil: he invited his hearers to repent (Luke 13:1–5). You see, sin is not just out there in the world—it is in each of our hearts. As Alexander Solzhenitsyn wrote in *The Gulag Archipelago:* "The line separating good and evil passes not through states, nor between classes, nor between political parties either—but right through every human heart."[15] Such is the beauty and brokenness of humanity.

One of the ways we express our concern over evil is through repentance and confession. We turn from our own sin. The world falls apart and relationships fracture when people refuse to admit they're wrong. That is why the philosopher Marilyn McCord Adams wrote, "Continual repentance is not only necessary for the

Christian's own reconciliation with Christ, but also the best contribution he can make towards solving the problem of evil."[16] As Christians, we refuse to participate in evil by owning our part in it. After all, there is something off-putting about demanding that God clean up the world but refusing to let him start in us!

Though the skeptic might state that if God were good and powerful he would eliminate evil and suffering, the Christian response is: God is good, God is powerful, and God *will* eliminate evil. God is patient, not wanting anyone to perish. God intends to get rid of evil without getting rid of us, so

> As Christians, we refuse to participate in evil by owning our part in it.

he invites us to lay down our arms and join his side freely. But this, of course, requires us to humbly admit our own contributions to the problem of evil.

So, please, be concerned about the evil in the world. But also be concerned about the evil within.

A second practical way to respond to the problem of evil is to enter into suffering like Jesus did. The importance of this can be seen in a university study on pain endurance. The researchers had a person come into a room by themselves and stand in a bucket filled with ice. They timed the participants to see how long they could endure the freezing cold. What they found was that, across the board, when the participant had a friend with them in the room it doubled the amount of pain they could endure. The researchers concluded that "the presence of another caring person doubles the amount of pain a person can endure."[17]

This is the ministry of presence. Sometimes in the midst of someone's pain it is easier to tell stories, offer advice, or extol the virtues of positive thinking—quote a Bible verse, share a mini-devotional, and then move on. Those things can be easier than just sitting with someone in their grief. Sitting seems almost useless and unproductive, but our presence is a gift.[18]

Neonatal pediatrician Dr. John Wyatt works with babies in distress, and sometimes there are no treatments left for his tiny patients. His expertise runs out. It is then that Wyatt simply sits and weeps with the grieving parents. He writes, "Suffering in another human being is a call to the rest of us to stand in community, it is a call to be there. Suffering is not a question which demands an answer, it is not a problem which requires a solution, it is a mystery which demands a presence."[19]

Jesus entered into our suffering to remind us that we are not alone and that we are not forsaken. We are to do the same. Enter into suffering rather than shy away. Practice a ministry of presence that doesn't minimize pain but provides support through the difficult season. In the words of Gregory Coles, "The truest friends I've ever known are the ones who offer me more than answers. The ones who sit in the ashes and allow me to weep and share in my sorrow. The ones who embrace God's riddles with me."[20] These are the types of friends we are called to be.

> Enter into suffering rather than shy away. Practice a ministry of presence that doesn't minimize pain but provides support through the difficult season.

We have been sent by Jesus into this broken and hurting world to bind up the brokenhearted and wipe away tears. The New Testament teaches that when we join ourselves to Christ through faith, we become the hands and feet of Jesus, the body of Christ in the world, so when people are hurting and asking, "Where is God?" there the church must be.

God's answer to evil and suffering was the person of Jesus Christ. Our answer must be to become a people committed to Jesus and passionately pursuing the alleviation of hurt and pain in his name, binding up the brokenhearted, providing hope for those who feel hopeless, and making the prayer of St. Francis our own:

Lord, make me an instrument of your peace.
Where there is hatred, let me sow love;
where there is injury, pardon;
where there is doubt, faith;
where there is despair, hope;
where there is darkness, light;
where there is sadness, joy.

Amen.

5. Are Faith and Science in Conflict?

KIRK DURSTON

One golden autumn at the age of eighteen, motivated by an impossible dream of being the first man on Mars, I began a degree in physics at the University of Manitoba. Within a few months, I had the worship-inspiring experience of gazing on the delicate pastel rings of Saturn with my own eyes through a university telescope. At the end of my second year, I landed my first science-related summer job with the Manitoba Geological Survey doing geological mapping. Upon completing my undergraduate degree in physics, I moved on to complete a degree in mechanical engineering. My final summer job as a student was for National Defence Research in Esquimalt, British Columbia, writing software to detect

Soviet submarines. Eventually, my lifetime love of science led me to a PhD in biophysics, along with publications in academic journals of science. My passion for science has always gone hand in hand with my love of God and his creation.

But not everyone has had the same experience. One of my favorite sci-fi authors during my high school years was Arthur C. Clarke. In his book *Childhood's End*, the character Karellen states, "Science can destroy religion by ignoring it as well as by disproving its tenets."[1] Having walked the halls of science for many years, and having talked with many hundreds of university students, I am well aware of the tension between science and faith. There is a widespread perception that whenever science and faith come into conflict, it is faith in science that must take precedence. Science, so popular thinking goes, is our beacon of truth. The reality, however, is quite a different story.

What do you do when you find yourself in a conversation with someone who believes that faith and science are at odds and chooses science? I will begin this chapter by presenting God as the foundation of science. I will then show why science can draw wrong conclusions about miraculous events. Next, I offer a critical exposé of modern science—the good, the shaky, and the downright bad. Finally, I will address two pitfalls against which the faithful must be on guard: the problem of assumed infallibility when it comes to one's understanding of Scripture, and the famous "God of the gaps" leap in logic sometimes taken by people of faith. The aim of this chapter is to show that pitting science against faith is a false choice.

GOD AS THE FOUNDATION OF SCIENCE

Christians believe that God created the universe and the laws of nature that govern it (Genesis 1:1; Job 38:33). Skeptics, of course, may not grant this, but logic is against them. For example, the consensus among physicists is that a beginning to the universe is unavoidable.[2] This raises a problem: what caused the universe (which we will call *nature*)?

Logic permits only two options: the cause of nature must be either natural (entirely dependent on space, time, matter, and energy) or not-natural (that is, supernatural). However, just as a woman cannot give birth to herself, so nature cannot give birth to itself—that would be a case of circular reasoning and logically impossible. So, to quote Sherlock Holmes, "Once you eliminate the impossible,

> The very foundation of nature and science is supernatural.

whatever remains, no matter how improbable, must be the truth." Logic dictates, therefore, that when faced with the choice between nature giving birth to itself, or a non-natural, supernatural cause, the natural option must be eliminated. The supernatural option "must be the truth."

Therefore, *the very foundation of nature and science is supernatural.* The physical world (nature) was caused by, and exists within, a larger, supernatural context. This is not a religious assertion; deductive logic and rational thinking entail it. So, given that logic requires a supernatural foundation for science and the universe, what is the role of science?

The laws of nature God has created provide consistency, repeatability, and predictability for natural processes. This is what makes science possible. *Science is our tool to study how nature works.*

And God encourages science. As one of the psalms states:

Great are the works of the Lord;
    they are pondered by all who delight in them.
    (Psalm 111:2)

The earliest recorded scientist is King Solomon in ancient Israel, approximately 2,900 years ago. Of him it is written in the Bible,

> God gave Solomon wisdom and very great insight, and a breadth of understanding as measureless as the sand on the seashore. He spoke about plant life, from the cedar of Lebanon to the hyssop that grows out of walls. He also spoke about animals and birds, reptiles and fish. From all nations people came to listen to Solomon's wisdom, sent by all the kings of the world, who had heard of his wisdom.
> (1 Kings 4:29, 33–34)

The study of God's creation has continued down throughout the millennia. Some famous scientists who regarded themselves as Christians include: Francis Bacon, Galileo, Blaise Pascal, Isaac Newton, Johannes Kepler, Carl Linnaeus, Michael Faraday, Charles Babbage, James Clerk Maxwell, Gregor Mendel, Louis Pasteur, Lord

Kelvin, Charles Doolittle Walcott, Max Planck, George Washington Carver, Arthur Eddington, Georges Lemaître, Theodosius Dobzhansky, Werner Heisenberg, James Tour, Freeman Dyson, Francis Collins, John Polkinghorne, and John Lennox—and these are only a few of the more well-known scientists who have professed a Christian faith. I personally know of many more, currently teaching in universities around the world, engaging in research, and publishing in journals of science.

Just yesterday I read a comment by an atheist who listed several natural phenomena that science has explained, concluding from them that there is no need for God. But the ability of science to explain how nature works is exactly what we would expect if God has created laws of nature that make science possible. It is a mistake, therefore, to think that because science can explain how nature works that it has somehow explained away the need for God. Quite the contrary! God, and the laws of nature he created, provide science's foundation.

Unfortunately, some conclude that the regularity we observe in nature rules out miracles, but this does not logically follow at all.

THE CHALLENGE OF MIRACLES

G. K. Chesterton once quipped, "The most incredible thing about miracles is that they happen."[3] If, as we just saw, logic requires a supernatural origin and foundation for the natural world, the burden is actually on the person who asserts that miracles are *not* an option to provide justification for the belief that the supernatural foundation of nature would never be evident within the natural world. Given that nature requires a supernatural foundation, it would be surprising if the supernatural never interacted within the physical world.

But what exactly is a miracle? A miracle can be broadly defined as an event for which the laws of physics were not entirely sufficient. For many events that occur in this world, it may be impossible to determine if it was a miracle or not. For example, let's say elderly Aunt

> A miracle can be broadly defined as an event for which the laws of physics were not entirely sufficient.

Mabel has the flu and her natural immune system will not be sufficient to save her, *but we do not have that foreknowledge.* I ask God to heal Aunt Mabel of the flu and, within a few days, she recovers.

Now, natural processes heal people of the flu all the time. But in this particular case, and unbeknownst to me, those processes would not have been enough on their own without the additional intervention of God. Aunt Mabel's recovery would appear to be perfectly natural, even though divine involvement took place. The implication is that nature is sufficiently complex that this type of miracle could be occurring thousands of times over per day and *we would never know it*. With this in mind, prayer may be more important than we realize.

Then there are events where natural processes are obviously insufficient, and we can, with a high degree of confidence, conclude they are miracles. For example, if Jesus took five loaves and two small fish, fed five thousand people with them, and had twelve baskets of fish and bread left over, natural processes are inadequate on several levels. Yet if, as we have already seen, physical reality has a supernatural foundation, it should not be surprising at all if there are supernatural interactions within the physical world.

Now for a cautionary note: we must be careful of science's assessment of miraculous events. For example, at a wedding in Cana, Jesus turned water into "very good" wine. If we sent that wine off to several labs to ask if this wine could have been produced from water in a matter of seconds, unanimous scientific consensus could supply two reasons why this was impossible. First, new wine requires about a year, not seconds, to produce the chemical compounds required. Second, wine requires carbon compounds, but there is no carbon in water—just hydrogen and oxygen. To produce carbon would require fission of the oxygen atoms in the water jars, producing a nuclear holocaust that would probably end the wedding prematurely. Our scientists would therefore conclude that wine can be produced naturally without requiring a miracle, so the biblical account cannot be taken at face value.

But they would be wrong, because they don't account for intervention by an outside force. This makes all the difference. For example, technology is drawing closer to the point where we may be able to produce self-driving cars controlled by sophisticated software. But we can also build into that system the option for the driver to override the self-driving controls or intervene to do something special or unusual that the software is not designed to do. The Christian understanding of miracles is that, in exactly the same way, if God designed the laws of nature to "self-drive" the universe, he can still intervene to perform special events the normal laws are not designed to do. Self-driving cars and the universe can both permit intervention by a person equipped to do so.

MODERN SCIENCE: THE GOOD, THE SHAKY, AND THE BAD

Recently, I read an article extolling the trustworthiness of science because it is evidence-based and employs "intense scrutiny."[4] While science certainly can lead us to truth, the reality is more complicated than is often assumed. It would perhaps be helpful to divide what is popularly called "science" into three different categories: experimental science, inference science, and fantasy science. The results of the first category are trustworthy much of the time. The results of the second category are sometimes trustworthy, and sometimes not. As for the third category—well, not so much.

EXPERIMENTAL SCIENCE

All of science's contributions to humanity, such as aircraft, smartphones, huge advances in medicine, and vaccines that have saved the lives of millions have come from experimental science. Over my years in the sciences, I have never encountered any challenges to faith that have emerged from this kind of science. It sticks to what we call the *scientific method*, which includes experimentally reproducing or verifying its theories and predictions.

Falsifiable predictions are what keep scientific theories accountable to reality; these can be experimentally tested, verified, or falsified. Those of us

> While science certainly can lead us to truth, the reality is more complicated than is often assumed.

who have listened to various conspiracy theories know that one can cobble together what looks like evidence for even the wildest theory. Falsification, however, is the referee's whistle for bogus theories. It shows that, despite what *appears* to be evidence, the idea cannot be right. Experimental verification and reproducibility keep science accountable.

Experimental science sticks to the scientific method. The key predictions have been tested and verified, the data collected, and actual results obtained and published in peer-reviewed science journals. Independent testing has obtained the same results using the same methods. For example, it is an experimental fact that variation occurs within different species and natural selection can weed out certain varieties, leaving those that are better at reproducing. We can call this "micro" evolution, and it clearly falls into verified experimental science; it is repeatable and verifiable.

Experimental science is one of the most trustworthy endeavors we engage in, but even in this realm human nature has spread its corrupting influence. In 2012, one of the most prestigious science journals in the world revealed a study that it described as "shocking." Fifty-three "landmark" papers in the area of cancer research were sent to independent labs to confirm the findings claimed in the paper. Only six could be reproduced; an astonishing 89 percent failed to be confirmed.[5] Six years later, another article in the same journal stated, "Since then [referring to the 2012 article], numerous studies (most recently in psychology and cancer biology) have confirmed that failure to replicate published findings is the norm."[6] This means the disturbing discovery in 2012 was not an isolated incident;

> Experimental science is one of the most trustworthy endeavors we engage in, but even in this realm human nature has spread its corrupting influence.

it is normal in at least the biological sciences. The reason given in the article was that "in the competitive crucible of modern science, various perverse incentives conspire to undermine the scientific method, leading to a literature littered with unreliable findings." In other words, scientists experience pressure to publish positive findings. This pressure comes from a desire for funding, academic prestige, and security, as well as philosophical commitments to certain theories. Consequently, human nature coupled with "perverse incentives" work together to corrupt even experimental science.

If even experimental science, where there is a very high potential for accountability, can be corrupted by human nature, we need to exercise great caution before citing the "latest study." Even so, I am not aware of anything in the category of experimental science that poses a challenge to faith. The tension begins in the next category of science.

INFERENCE SCIENCE

This category takes the results of experimental science, which are observable and reproducible, but then adds extrapolations and assumptions to explain things that we are not in a position to reproduce experimentally. The results range from reliable to completely untrustworthy.

Forensic science is an example of reliable inference science. Police detectives and laboratories cannot reproduce the event, but they can gather evidence and test it. A good investigation will go where the evidence points, but that inductive step is usually not very large if it is to stand up in a court of law.

Much bigger leaps, however, must be taken when reconstructing the history of the universe or the history of life. In these cases, the inductive leaps can be many, with a mix of small and large. The conclusions should be held with the greatest of caution. The history of the universe depends on substantial assumptions and untested theories, and science's reconstruction is not nearly as trustworthy as the general public has been led to believe.

For example, an essential component of the current big bang theory is a brief but powerful period of rapid inflation of space-time, which should have produced gravity waves that can be detected today. Although our gravity wave detectors have grown so sensitive that we can detect collisions between stars, it is striking that we have been unable to detect gravity waves from a theoretical rapid inflation near the beginning of the universe.[7] In general, the bigger the inference or assumption, the more tentatively we should hold it.

The primary threat to the integrity of modern science is scientism. *Scientism* is the belief that science explains everything.[8] It is a philosophical commitment that can't be arrived at through scientific inquiry. Essentially, it is atheism dressed up in a lab coat, requiring modern science to *a priori* rule out any possible involvement of God in the origin of the universe and of life, reinterpreting any evidence that might point toward God. Unfortunately, scientism has a significant influence upon the inductive inferences science makes today. Not surprisingly, most of the tension between faith and science arises from the influence of scientism in modern science.

> The primary threat to the integrity of modern science is scientism. *Scientism* is the belief that science explains everything.

Perhaps no other area of science has been so heavily dependent on scientism-motivated, creative storytelling as the origin and diversity of life. We have an enormous amount of experimental evidence, of course, for the small-scale evolution of things like finch beaks, Pepper moths, viral strains, and antibiotic-resistant bacteria—all more accurately described as *variation*—but theories of large-scale, common descent are a very different matter.

Jerry Fodor and Massimo Piattelli-Palmarini, both of whom are committed to Darwinian evolution, wrote,

> Much of the vast neo-Darwinian literature is distressingly uncritical. The possibility that anything is seriously amiss with Darwin's account of evolution is hardly considered. ... The methodological skepticism that characterizes most areas of scientific discourse seems strikingly absent when Darwinism is the topic.[9]

Our total, ongoing failure to reproduce large-scale evolution in the lab, despite thousands of scientists performing intelligently guided, selective breeding experiments that should speed up the process by many orders of magnitude, should be deeply disturbing—to the point of calling into question whether such a process is even possible. The central testable prediction of large-scale evolution is that there should be no limits to variation, a prediction not borne out by experimental science. In every experiment to date where we try to push the limits, we always hit a wall, no exceptions. Quite simply, we do not run out of time; we run into the limits of the digital information encoded in the genomes of life. Inducing mutations to speed up the process results in accumulating genetic damage. Normally in science, we do not accept a conclusion as fact until we have replicated it. Perhaps the single greatest "elephant in the room" in the history of science is its vehement acceptance of the "fact" of blind and mindless common descent in the face of science's continual failure to replicate it in intelligently guided and accelerated experiments. Under the influence of scientism, the belief that all of life arose through blind and mindless processes is simply "too big to fail."

In inference science, when the inductive leaps become large, the lack of supporting data is often made up for with what can be called "lack-of-data words" or "wishful thinking phrases." At one point in my PhD research, my supervisor noticed a statement in the conclusion of a paper I was submitting to a journal that went something like, "These results suggest ... " He looked at me and asked, "Suggests? Do you have data to support that?" I allowed that I did not; it was only an inference. He then suggested I remove such speculation from my paper unless

I had the data to support it. Such lack-of-data words are commonplace in evolutionary biology when researchers begin to construct a narrative about how life evolved. For example, in the two-page article "The Origin of the Very First Species and the Start of Darwinian Evolution," there are twenty-eight lack-of-data words and phrases, including "presumably," "probably," "possible," "might have," "at some time," "possible scenario," "could have," "proposed," "over time," "eventually generated," "researchers believe," "seems likely," "is conceivable," "incidentally coincided," and "potentially."[10] We need to train ourselves to watch out for lack-of-data words when reading the latest science article. Once we start noticing them, we can begin to sort good inference science from extrapolations that involve huge leaps augmented by creative words and phrases.

FANTASY SCIENCE

This third category represents modern science at its worst. It occurs when scientists make up theories that cannot be tested experimentally. Many of us have encountered science news stories that enthrall us with the possibility that our universe is just one of a bubbling froth of universes called the *multiverse*, or articles claiming that the universe was actually produced by nothing. These mind-blowing ideas have been much touted in the popular media, but there is no way to test them. Worse still, such theories are a threat to the "integrity of physics" and "undermine science," argue applied mathematician George Ellis and cosmologist Joe Silk.[11] Quite simply, they are science fiction masquerading as science, which is why I call them "fantasy science."

> Modern science has become a mix of good science, bad science, creative storytelling, science fiction, scientism, citation-bias, huge media announcements followed by quiet retractions, massaging the data, exaggeration for funding purposes, and outright fraud, all rolled up into one thing that is misleadingly called "science."

In short, modern science has become a mix of good science, bad science, creative storytelling, science fiction, scientism, citation-bias, huge media announcements followed by quiet retractions, massaging the data, exaggeration for funding purposes, and outright fraud, all rolled up into one thing that is misleadingly called "science." In some disciplines, the problem has become so rampant that the good science is drowning in a mess of everything else.[12]

If all of this has shaken your faith in science, a wee bit of damage control is in order. There are many good scientists committed to the highest standards of integrity, carefully practicing science. Remember that some of the landmark cancer-research papers mentioned above *could* be reproduced. My advice to students who are interested in a science career is that they aspire to a noble, God-honoring venture, but they should commit to the practice of impeccable science, maintaining scientific integrity amidst the "perverse incentives" they will encounter.

The scientific method and experimental science are very trustworthy and pose no challenge to faith. The so-called conflict between faith and science comes out of theories that have never actually been reproduced in a lab. The sad thing is that some who grew up in the church jump ship on the basis of scientism-driven scenarios that depend on creative stories and lack-of-data words, huge extrapolations and inductive leaps, with essential predictions that are either falsified or have yet to be successfully tested. We need to exercise the same healthy skepticism for scientific claims and their creative stories and scenarios as we do for anything else.

It is not just science that has some issues, however. Christians can make mistakes as well.

DOES SCIENCE CONTRADICT THE BIBLE?

While enthusiasts of popular science can quickly leap to inferences about the origins of life without proper grounding in the scientific method, Christians can make a similar overconfident leap when it comes to Bible interpretation. For example, I often see Christians who are utterly confident that their interpretation of Genesis 1 is absolutely infallible. Yet within the church, and long before Charles Darwin, there have been a variety of different understandings of Genesis held by theologians like Origen (ca. AD 220), Augustine (ca. AD 400),

> I often see Christians who are utterly confident that their interpretation of Genesis 1 is absolutely infallible.

and Thomas Aquinas (ca. AD 1250). Regardless of our understanding of Genesis 1, we need to be humble and cautious in our approach. Given the many different interpretations of Genesis 1 throughout the Christian tradition, instead of taking an overly confident position on the exact nature of the days or the age of the earth, it might be better to say, "I lean toward this understanding over that one for reasons I can explain, but I realize the Bible says some things that make me cautious about insisting I am unquestioningly right in my interpretation." When dealing with a person who assumes faith and science are opposed to each other, a bit of humility goes a long way.

It is also perfectly fine to say "I don't know" when pressed to respond to some perceived conflict between the Bible and science. We may simply not have sufficient information about some things to resolve every apparent problem or challenge. God knows the details completely; we may not. Sometimes the most honest response we can give is to admit we do not feel sufficiently qualified to resolve the issue, or even comment on it.

There is one more problem that frequently surfaces in discussions of God and science. Just as inference science and fantasy science can take unjustified leaps that cannot be proven via experimental science, and Christians can assume the infallibility of their own interpretation of Genesis 1, so Christians can also take leaps in logic when they invoke God for something that they cannot explain.

THE GOD-OF-THE-GAPS PROBLEM

A few years ago, my expensive Gore-Tex snow pants vanished from my closet. I ransacked the house, searching high and low several times over many months, but have never found an explanation for their disappearance. If I were to therefore conclude that God did it, I would be making a shaky assumption, since a perfectly good explanation that didn't require divine intervention might surface next week.

When we assume God did something when we have no other explanation, we are invoking the "God of the gaps." The premise we use looks like this:

If we do not know what caused X, then God did it.

When considering such an argument, there are three things to keep in mind. First, a God-of-the-gaps argument does not *automatically* lead to a false conclusion—it may well be the case that the event was a miracle. But second, the danger of such an argument is that a perfectly natural explanation may be discovered at some point in the future, to the embarrassment of those

> When we assume God did something when we have no other explanation, we are invoking the "God of the gaps."

who thought it was a miracle. Third, the God-of-the-gaps argument is based on what we *do not* know rather than on what we *do* know. Because of the possibility that we may find a perfectly natural explanation at some point in the future, it is better to look for positive reasons to support the conclusion.

Let's take a look at two examples of God-of-the-gaps arguments and their solutions. The first is the origin of the universe. A God-of-the-gaps argument could be summarized as, "We don't know what caused the universe; therefore, God did it." The person who makes this argument may actually be right about God creating the universe, but the argument is based on the absence of knowledge rather than on something that we know.

A better argument that does not require God-of-the-gaps reasoning could be stated as follows:

1. The cause of the universe is either natural or supernatural (i.e., not-natural).

2. It is logically impossible for the cause of the universe (i.e., nature) to be natural.

3. Therefore, the cause of the universe is supernatural.

The first premise is a true dichotomy; there are only two mutually exclusive options to choose from. The second premise is required by logic in order to avoid the circular fallacy; after all, a woman cannot give birth to herself. The argument, therefore, is better than the God-of-the-gaps version because it is based on what we know—in this case, what we know about logical inference. The questionable gaps premise, "We don't know what caused the universe," is nowhere used in the argument.

The second example has to do with the origin of life. A God-of-the-gaps argument could be summarized as, "We don't know what produced the functional information encoded in the DNA of the first life form; therefore, God did it." Once again, it may be true that God created life, but the argument is based on the absence of knowledge regarding what can produce meaningful or functional information. Thus, it is also a God-of-the-gaps argument.

A solution that does not rely on God-of-the-gaps reasoning could be described in this way:

1. The only thing ever observed by science that can produce significant levels of meaningful/functional information is an intelligent mind.

2. The DNA of the simplest life form required significant levels of functional information.

3. Therefore, the functional information in the simplest life form was produced by an intelligent mind.

Interestingly, scientists committed by scientism to avoid invoking the existence of a Creator have their own God-of-the-gaps-style argument: a multiverse. The odds of the universe being fine-tuned to support life are so infinitesimally small that, rather than admit to the existence of an intelligent creator, some have invoked a near-infinite number of universes to explain the existence of this universe. Scientist George Ellis has pointed out that the motive for proposing many universes is not because there is any scientific evidence for them, but to try to explain away the fantastic improbability of a universe designed to support life.[13] Some scientists have conceded that the chance of life appearing anywhere at all in this universe is so outrageously small that we should never expect it to happen. Therefore, a near-infinite number of universes is proposed to solve that wild improbability.[14] We could call this a "multiverse-of-the-gaps," in which scientists are appealing to a near-infinite number of unseen, untestable entities in order to avoid having to admit that the possibility of one unseen, intelligent creator behind the universe and life. Ockham's razor, the principle that suggests we shouldn't unnecessarily multiply explanatory entities when a single, simple explanation will do, indicates that we should go with one unseen creator rather than a near-infinite number of imaginary universes.

The takeaway, for both Christians and skeptics, is to avoid making an argument based on what we do not know. It is better to base an argument on what we do know or what is plausible from history, logic, mathematics, science, and so forth.

CONCLUSION

Probably the single greatest source of tension between God and science is neither God nor science, but scientism: atheism posing as science. God, as the creator of nature and the laws that govern it, has provided a foundation for us to learn about the universe using the scientific method. Science is our tool to figure out how nature works. Rigorous experimental science does not pose a challenge to faith. In the end, what science has *actually* shown to be true is radically less than what the general public, including some theologians, *believe* it has shown.

To the everyday Christian I say two final things. First, be appropriately humble in your understanding of what Scripture teaches before assuming that your reading of Scripture is infallible. There may be information you have not yet noticed, or are unaware of, or have not taken seriously, or have not thought deeply enough about.

> Probably the single greatest source of tension between God and science is neither God nor science, but scientism: atheism posing as science.

Second, don't be intimidated by claims that science and faith are enemies. There are far too many Christians intimidated on the basis of untested, un-reproduced, and un-duplicated scientific scenarios. Instead, practice integrity, humility, and careful thinking in both faith and science, and you may be surprised at how science can move you to worship your Creator as well as enrich your life.

In the end, science—properly done, using the scientific method—is a noble pursuit, pleasing and glorifying to God.

6. How Can We Reconcile the Exclusive Claims of Christ with a Pluralistic Culture?

JASON BALLARD

I once heard a joke that started, "A Christian, a Buddhist, an atheist, and a Muslim all walk into a bar together ... " To be honest, I can't remember the punch line, but I do remember thinking, "That sounds like a Friday night in Vancouver."

One of my favorite things about living in the Pacific Northwest is the cultural diversity represented in a city like Vancouver, British Columbia. I experienced this up close every day as an undergraduate studying at Simon Fraser University. Each classroom was a stunning picture of cultural diversity—a wide spectrum of beliefs, religious convictions, and cultural perspectives all together experiencing the freedom and respect afforded in a pluralistic society.

In an English class, I once listened to an engaging and somewhat tense discussion surrounding the questions of pluralism and exclusivity. Reflecting on an outspoken Christian character in the book our class had been reading, one classmate claimed that it was arrogant and unkind for people to believe that their religious beliefs are absolutely true. More specifically, she rejected this claim because of the implication that those who disagree are wrong.

> At its core, the question behind the problem of exclusivity is: "How can any person claim to know *the* truth about God to the exclusion of all other truth claims?"

This is not a unique frustration. It shows up in all kinds of different ways and is often labeled as the *problem of exclusivity*. At its core, the question behind this problem is: "How can any person claim to know *the* truth about God to the exclusion of all other truth claims?" In the place of "God," you could also substitute eternal life, heaven, the good life, the full life, utopia, or enlightenment. However you might describe it, the problem of exclusivity is the problem of absolute truth and whether any individual can claim access to it. As more and more of us live in places with cultural diversity like Vancouver, Christians run into this problem a lot. How can we respond?

Before getting into how to address the logic behind the problem of exclusivity, first I want to acknowledge that most discussions of this question are also driven by the emotional and social implications lying underneath the surface.

THE ROOTS OF OUR AVERSION

Some of you may be familiar with the Enneagram. Put simply, it posits that there are nine unique personality types, and each type tries to capture the common root desire of each human being. For some it's success; others, perfection; and for still others, peace. My wife identifies as a Nine: the Peacemaker. Peacemakers seek to avoid tension and conflict in order to maintain harmony in the world around them and resist anything that might compromise their sense of inner peace.

If Canada, where I live, could be identified with an Enneagram type, it would also be a Nine. And while many of us might be more comfortable with conflict than an Enneagram Nine, there is a deep cultural current in the

Western world that is conflict-averse. As a result, the very nature of exclusive truth claims challenges our emotional sensibilities. In an attempt to preserve the peace, we (all of us, not just Canadians) avoid our religious differences or pretend they don't exist.

Our culture's aversion to exclusive truth claims is not only rooted in the fear of conflict. Often, we find ourselves opposed to exclusive truth claims because we feel that these types of beliefs are, by their very nature, unloving and unkind.

More and more it seems that people think loving someone means accepting everything about them, and that includes all of their ideas. To

It is only when we turn down the volume on our fear and reject our mistaken definition of love that we can truly tackle the problem of exclusivity.

disagree with someone's ideas feels akin to disagreeing with the person as a whole. In other words, we find it difficult to embrace people with ideas or beliefs that we don't ourselves hold. If we don't agree with them, it means we don't accept them; therefore, how could we possibly love them?

In the minds of many today, both the fear of conflict and the mistaken idea that loving people requires affirming the validity of all of their ideas amplify the offense of holding to exclusive religious views. It is only when we turn down the volume on our fear and reject our mistaken definition of love that we can truly tackle the problem of exclusivity. The challenging question becomes, "How do we do this? How do we turn down the fear and dial up the love?" In the pages that follow I will help us chart a course through the choppy waters created by this cultural objection. I will explore how the Christian worldview addresses both the faulty logic and the underlying fear that provides fuel for this objection.

ALL PATHS DON'T LEAD TO GOD

I have three children. Hudson, my oldest, is five, and his best friend, Lincoln, lives next door. They love to race in our backyard, and Hudson hates to lose. I am not going to lie: when the race is close, I often say, "You both won."

This tactic worked really well when they were younger, but recently they caught on to me, and now my go-to line no longer cuts it. "Dad, we can't both win! That's impossible." Hudson hasn't taken any university courses on logic, but he already has a healthy grasp on the nature of truth and mutual exclusivity.

If you have ever had to settle disputes between col-leagues at work, you might have tried a similar approach. Instead of taking sides in an argument, you pull this card out of your back pocket: "You are both right." It is the adult version of "You both win!"

In the conversation about religious beliefs, this is also a popular response. Many people live surrounded by indi-viduals with different religious affiliations and beliefs. So, instead of disturbing the peace by claiming that everyone is wrong, or at least everyone is wrong except those who hold a particular viewpoint, why not say that everyone is right?

There are all kinds of metaphors and stories that are told to convey this idea in the religious space, whether it be blind men grabbing onto different parts of an ele-phant, or different paths ending at the top of the same mountain. The point is simple: everyone is just holding on to a part of the same truth, without any individual able to claim that they see the full picture. Once we remove our blindfolds and somehow step outside the picture to a higher vantage point, we find that we are all actually talking about the same thing.

This approach is appealing. Everyone wins and no one loses. But does it actually work? Does this actually promote peace and love in the way intended?

NO ONE ACTUALLY BELIEVES ALL PATHS LEAD TO GOD

The problem is that no one actually believes that all paths lead to God. I know it might sound unfair or cheeky to suggest this when you are talking with someone who is presenting this argument, but once you take a close look at this idea, it falls apart really quickly.

In the marketplace of religious ideas, there are extreme religious beliefs that most people in the West have no problem rejecting or declaring to be untrue. Consider those religious traditions that require child sacrifice or girls being forcibly mutilated. Or how about the extremist who believes that the path to paradise is blowing up innocent people? Most people, even those who normally say that all paths lead to God, would say that these are in fact not equally valid paths to God.

Once we acknowledge this, we are confronted with a dilemma: Should we say instead that *most* religions lead to

God, but not all? If so, how many should we exclude? And if we are going to exclude some and not others, what criteria should we use to decide? Who gets to decide which moral framework or worldview we use to determine which "truths" are not as legitimate as others?

Matters are too complex to pass around simple catchphrases like "all roads lead to God," especially just to avoid an accusation of exclusivity. There are religious and cultural beliefs that have been used consistently to marginalize specific ethnicities and to justify horrible atrocities throughout history. As a Christian, I reject those beliefs. I do not think those are equally valid ways of viewing the world. And I am sure most people, regardless of their religious viewpoint, would agree.

> Matters are too complex to pass around simple catchphrases like "all roads lead to God," especially just to avoid an accusation of exclusivity.

This is why truth matters. And when making any truth claim about the world, the nature of God, or what makes for the good life, people will *in that very act* exclude contrary beliefs. This is just the nature of making truth claims about the world. And the reality is that all religions do this very thing. And it is not just religious viewpoints that do this, but also ideologies and worldviews that reject belief in God. After all, to confidently assert that God does not exist dismisses all theistic belief systems as wrong-headed and false.

THE LAW OF NON-CONTRADICTION

Everyone intuitively knows what logicians have called *the law of non-contradiction*. Here's how it works: If premise 1 claims A is B, and premise 2 states that A is not B, the two premises contradict each other. Both cannot be true. A cannot be B and not-B at the same time and in the same sense.

To illustrate this practically, if premise 1 states that a piece of fruit is an apple, and premise 2 states the same piece of fruit is an orange, you cannot say both premises are true. It is one or the other; it cannot be both. The very nature of a truth-claim like "this is an apple" necessarily implies that you are also saying, "this is not an orange." Of course, when we are talking about apples and oranges, we are not afraid of offending others. But this principle helps us sort through religious beliefs and provides us with another reason why, logically speaking, not all religions can be true.

Certain strands of Buddhism believe that there is no God, whereas Muslims believe there is only one God (Allah) and Muhammad is his prophet. Both can be wrong, but both can certainly not be right. Jewish people believe that Jesus is not the Messiah and Savior promised by the Old Testament. Christians believe that Jesus *is* the Messiah and Savior promised by the Old Testament. Again, the law of non-contradiction tells us that both cannot possibly be true.

Christians, Muslims, and Jews believe in one Creator God. Atheists believe in no God. If the atheist is right about reality, Christians, Jewish people, and Muslims are wrong, which means that, in one sense, even the atheist holds an exclusive religious belief.

There are several conclusions we can draw from this. First, the statement that all religions are true, or all paths lead to God, is a logical impossibility. Second, much of the world's population would consider themselves part of a religion that holds to exclusive beliefs about reality. As I said above, this is just the nature of making truth claims about the world. Third, while claiming that "all religions are true or are ultimately the same" sounds like a kind and accommodating statement on the surface, in reality it can be deeply offensive and arrogant. To say to Muslims that they ultimately believe the same thing as Buddhists is to insinuate that what they believe is trivial. It is implying that the actual content of their beliefs is unimportant and interchangeable. In many ways it is imposing an alien, pluralistic view of religion, held by a small minority of people in recent history, on all these

> To say to Muslims that they ultimately believe the same thing as Buddhists is to insinuate that what they believe is trivial.

ancient and diverse religious traditions, emptying them of the actual meaning they hold for their adherents and devotees. That is both arrogant and exclusive. In an effort to accommodate everyone, we find ourselves excluding and offending almost everyone.

There is, however, another way to categorize religious truth claims that would potentially avoid the above problems. Perhaps when people claim that all religions are true, what they actually mean is that all religions are true for the people who believe in them. Could it be that Christianity, and all the major world religions, are not operating in the realm of objective truth and for that reason the arguments above are invalid? What if religious belief is the kind of truth that is unique to the individual?

In other words, perhaps religion only deals with subjective truth.

SUBJECTIVE AND OBJECTIVE TRUTH

When someone claims they are cold, is that statement true? Well, assuming they're not lying, yes. Now, what if the person beside them replies, "I am hot!"? This exact scenario plays out for my wife and me on road trips all the time. Now, who is telling the truth? Both could be accurately describing their response to the environment because they are describing their subjective experience.

Some people argue that religious belief is like describing whether one is hot or cold. It is a personal experience, so we should not say who is right or wrong. Subjective truth is relative to the person or subject who is making the truth claim. When subjective truth reigns supreme, there are as many truths as there are people.

Subjective truth is unlike objective truth, which is truth that is independent of the person. If it is objectively true that it is raining outside, that remains true whether I believe it or not. Objective truth is not up for debate in a manner similar to subjective truth. Objective truth, when it comes to the temperature in the car, would be to say: "It is fifteen degrees Celsius in here." Whether one is hot or cold doesn't change that objective fact about the temperature.

So is religious truth objective or subjective? Christianity rejects the idea that religious beliefs live in the realm of subjective truth. Yes, Christians find their beliefs subjectively meaningful, but when I, or most Christians for that matter, claim that Jesus is the Savior of the world, or the way to God, I

> Christianity rejects the idea that religious beliefs live in the realm of subjective truth.

am making a truth claim: an objective fact that is true for me and true for you, whether everyone believes it or not.

The central event of the Christian faith is the bodily resurrection of Jesus Christ. Christians believe that Jesus rose from the dead, not metaphorically, but in history. There was an empty tomb, there were post-resurrection appearances, the lives of the disciples were changed, and eventually, the entire Roman Empire was transformed. All of it stems from not just a subjective belief on behalf of the first followers of Jesus, but an objective event that tells us something that is actually true about the world: God does exist, he intervened in human history as Jesus, sin can be forgiven, and death can be defeated. Since the resurrection is a historical event and not just a subjectively meaningful metaphor for believers, it is both vulnerable to falsification and able to be defended through historical evidence.

In other words, the resurrection of Jesus is an objective historical event; one that can be rejected or disputed, but not one that can be dismissed as just a personal, subjective belief.

HOW DO CHRISTIANS APPROACH OTHER RELIGIONS?

Christians believe that their faith is more than just subjectively meaningful; it is objectively true. We have already seen that these types of truth claims always exclude contrary views—there is no logical way to avoid this reality. This raises another set of very important questions, which express the emotional struggle many feel when we assume that since we are right, others are wrong: How should we think about other religious views? And how should we treat those who disagree with us?

C. S. Lewis, in his book *Mere Christianity*, really helped me think this issue through. He wrote:

If you are a Christian you do not have to believe that all the other religions are simply wrong all through. If you are an atheist you do have to believe that the main point in all the religions of the whole world is simply one huge mistake. If you are a Christian, you are free to think that all those religions, even the [strangest] ones, contain at least some hint of the truth. When I was an atheist I had to try to persuade myself that most of the human race have always been wrong about the questions that matter to them most; when I became a Christian I was able to take a more [generous] view. But of course, being a Christian does mean thinking that where Christianity differs from other religions, Christianity is right and they are wrong. As in arithmetic—there is only one right answer to a sum, and all other answers are wrong; but some of the wrong answers are much nearer being right than others.[1]

As Lewis points out, Christians are free to believe that there is truth in all kinds of religion. One does not have to dismiss other religions as completely wrong because there is often much that is good, beautiful, and true to be found in the various religious perspectives, which are followed by sincere people all around the world. The Bible makes sense of this because it tells us that everyone is made in the image of God, God gives every individual a conscience, and God has revealed himself in nature to all people.

> Christians are free to believe that there is truth in all kinds of religion.

This should lead us to expect that people will be religious, and that people's religious perspectives will overlap and find points of agreement, especially in regard to moral teaching. This is exactly what we find when we survey the world religions.

I recently sat beside a Muslim man on a plane who overheard me talking about fasting. As a Christian, I fast as a spiritual discipline. As a Muslim, this man had fasted much more than I have, so I learned a ton from my conversation with him. We discussed some of the practical benefits of fasting. At no point did we assume that we fundamentally agree on the nature of God or the identity of Christ, but we did find some commonality and were able to celebrate that fact.

My friend Chris has a similar story:

My neighbor Mohammed is a Muslim who loves to have lively discussions about faith and the nature of God. I am grateful that we have developed a very open relationship over the years, even to the point of being able to gently question or challenge one another's beliefs. One afternoon I wrote to Mohammed and asked him, "From your perspective, what must I do to be saved?" After providing me with a very thorough answer via email he quoted this Sura (chapter 2, verse 62) from the Koran as his own view. "Those who believe, and those who are Jewish, and the Christians, and the Sabeans—any who believe in God and the Last Day, and act righteously—will have their reward with their Lord; they have nothing to fear, nor will they grieve."

This passage from the Koran seemed to indicate that my friend believed that, as a Christian, I would be saved. From the little I knew about the Koran, I figured this was probably a controversial perspective within Islam, so I followed up with him over sushi. I asked if his perspective was universal in

Islam. He said "no," and, as I asked more questions, he finally said, "Here is what I think is true once you examine all the Koran has to say on this matter. I think that a Christian can be saved, provided they don't believe Jesus is the Son of God."

I responded to Mohammed by saying, "Mohammed, that is like saying a Christian can be saved provided they are not a Christian. That would be like me saying a Muslim can be saved provided they don't believe Mohammed is a prophet."

My friend burst out laughing, and I joined him as we both appreciated the implications of his statement. After the laughter died down, he said, rather sheepishly, "Well, I am just trying to tell you what the Koran says." I thanked him for his honesty, and our relationship continues to this day.

Chris and his neighbor had different religious views, but that didn't stop them from loving and celebrating one another. It didn't ruin their friendship; it just added an interesting, mutually enriching dynamic that allowed them both to grow. The story also illustrates the point that Lewis is making: as much as Chris had in common with his neighbor, for him to believe that Christ is the Son of God and Savior is to imply that Christianity is true. To deny its reality would be to embrace a false belief about God.

Before moving on, there is one other thing to note from Lewis. He points out that perhaps one of the most exclusive beliefs of all is to claim that you have the corner on truth by insisting that there is no God at all. When people insist that there is no God, or that believing in God is a delusion or virus of the mind, they are claiming that most of humanity throughout the course of history, and a huge percentage of the population today, are all dead wrong about the very belief that they may hold as most important of all.

But I have no problem with an atheist claiming that a huge percentage of the human population is wrong about God, and neither should you. It is the very nature of the conversation to suggest that not everyone is right. It is alright for an atheist to believe that Christians are wrong, and it is okay for a Muslim to believe that a Jewish person is wrong. It is even appropriate for a Christian to believe that a Hindu is wrong. And while we are at it, it is fair game for the Buddhist to think that we are all missing the point. In fact, as a Christian I want to defend the right for people to believe and think differently. When we make space for people to share their beliefs, while not dismissing them as trivial or subjective, we are, in that moment, treating them with dignity, love, and respect.

In the Christian view, here is what is not defensible: to reject a person on the basis of their religious affiliation alone. Disagreeing with an idea is never an excuse for acting dismissively toward a person. When we say

> Disagreeing with an idea is never an excuse for acting dismissively toward a person.

that someone has a false belief, we are not necessarily rejecting their friendship or implying that we don't appreciate them or value them as a person. This goes back to the fallacy mentioned at the beginning of the chapter. In our politically charged, divided society, we have started to act as though disagreement requires dismissal of the other. We can't stomach the discomfort of sitting at the table with people who hold different beliefs any longer.

To be a Christian is to resist this cultural tendency. To discover a picture of what this resistance looks like in reality, we only have to examine the life of Jesus. He both made claims of absolute truth about reality and was radically inclusive and loving toward tax collectors, prostitutes, and other first-century outcasts.

THE INCLUSIVE EXCLUSIVITY OF CHRISTIANITY

In the first century, the message of Christianity spread in a multicultural, spiritually pluralistic environment. In the midst of this cultural milieu the message of Jesus, as recorded in the New Testament, unapologetically presents Jesus as the only way to God.

In Acts 4, Peter and John, both disciples of Jesus, heal a man who has been crippled since birth. Peter proclaims that it was "by the name of Jesus of Nazareth" that he healed the man and goes on to say, "Salvation is found in no one else, for there is no other name under heaven given to mankind by which we must be saved." This statement confronts our cultural preferences around religious communication. It is so absolute and unaccommodating, so narrow and exclusive.

This belief goes farther back than the earliest Christians; it extends also to Jesus himself. In John 14:6 Jesus says, "I am the way and the truth and the life. No one comes to the Father except through me." Jesus is not

pulling any punches here; he is stating without compromise that he is the only path to God. The Christian conviction, based on this Scripture and others, is that Jesus is
the only way to God. He is the only way to salvation and
the good and full life that begins now and lasts forever.
And yet the claims of Christianity are the most inclusive
kind of exclusivity there is. How can this be?

The great Indian Christian Sadhu Sundar Singh was
a well-known evangelist in India. He once had a conversation with a professor of comparative religion from
the University of Cambridge. The professor asked him,
"What have you found in Christianity that you did not find
in your old religion?" Sadhu replied, "Professor, I have
found the dear Lord Jesus." The professor responded, "Oh
yes, I quite understand, but what particular principle or
doctrine? Tell me, what new philosophy have you found
in Christianity that you did not find in your old religion?"
And Sadhu patiently responded again, "Professor, I found
the Lord Jesus."[2]

Singh is getting at the heart of the Christian worldview. To be a Christian is to trust in Jesus and follow
in his ways. When we gaze at the person of Jesus, we
discover someone whose life is marked with the kind

of inclusivity that our culture longs to experience—an inclusivity that is supposed to be mirrored in the lives of his followers. Though Jesus had exclusive beliefs, he exhibited radically inclusive behavior and invited his followers to do the same. We must, like Jesus, advocate for a better way of living when we disagree with others about important matters—to love and defend and serve others without trying to erase the very real differences that still exist.

And yet, sadly, Christians are not always famous for this type of behavior. Gabe Lyons and David Kinnaman, in their book *unChristian*, take survey data from people living in the United States and conclude that some of the most common descriptors of Christians in

> Though Jesus had exclusive beliefs, he exhibited radically inclusive behavior and invited his followers to do the same.

America are "uncaring," "judgmental," and "hypocritical."[3] The tragedy is that a true understanding of Christian doctrine should lead to the opposite qualities in the life of Jesus' followers. When we seriously dig into Jesus' teachings, what he did and what he taught, we discover a liberating pathway through this tricky conversation about exclusivity—a pathway that is filled with grace, kindness, love, and truth. Not only that, we will find that the way of Jesus is our best shot at peace in the midst of all the competing worldviews, religious perspectives, and truth claims.

Here are some of the teachings of Jesus that I have found most helpful for navigating this conversation: First, the conviction that every person is made in the image of God. This should lead to radical love and value being assigned to each person. Second, the Christian teaching on sin and human depravity helps explain why people so often don't act as though other people are valuable and, instead, use their power to manipulate, exclude, or hurt others. And lastly, Christianity invites us to live a new life, modeled by Christ and empowered by the Holy Spirit. This invitation gives us hope for living as people who possess value and dignity as image bearers of God. In addition, it acts as profound motivation for treating others with that same dignity, value, and respect, because they also bear the image of God—no matter their religion or race.

One Christian priest in the Netherlands gave us a beautiful example of this. In 2004, a Muslim extremist killed Dutch filmmaker Theo van Gogh. In the days that followed the senseless attack, both churches and mosques became targets for retaliatory strikes, culminating in the bombing of an Islamic school. The violence and escalating tension shook a nation that prided itself on being open and tolerant.

At the moment of highest tension, Dutch Protestant minister Reverend Kees Sybrandi took a stand against the violence and hatred. He knocked on the door of his neighborhood mosque and told the Muslims gathered inside that he would stand guard outside every night until the attacks ceased. In the days that followed, this minister called on other churches to be involved, and they joined him in circling and guarding mosques for more than three months.

The pastor did not pretend that he believed all the same things as his Muslim friends. He didn't compromise his belief in the divinity of Christ and his literal death and resurrection as an objective fact about history.

Instead, when asked by curious journalists why he did this, Reverend Sybrandi replied, "Jesus. Jesus commanded me to love my neighbour; my enemy, too." In circling mosques and staying up all night to protect Muslim places of worship from violent attack, Sybrandi was following in the way of Jesus.[4]

Jesus was a force for peace in a divided world. Jesus confronted and rebuked those who marginalized others on the basis of race, religion, gender, or economic status. He included the broken, fragile, and excluded. The only question is whether we follow him and do the same.

CONCLUSION

One of my favorite accounts from the life of Jesus is his meeting with Zacchaeus. When Jesus invited Zacchaeus, a corrupt tax collector and a rejected member of society, to eat with him, he was inviting him into deep relationship. Sharing a meal was one of the most intimate acts of friendship that could be offered in that time. While the religious leaders scoffed at this gesture, Jesus was unfazed. This interaction with Zacchaeus illustrates the better way that Jesus came to show the world, a way in which we can enjoy close relationships with people who are different than us. In this way, Jesus' ministry pointed us toward God's promised and preferred future.

The finale of the Christian Scriptures paints a stirring picture of a wedding feast: at that feast is a table, and at that table are people from every tribe, tongue, and nation of the world. Everyone is invited to this feast because God has a big table and there is room for all. This is God's promised future, and he invites us to bring his future into our present, making it a reality in our broken and divided world. Therefore, Christians need to be passionately against anything that shatters the peace that God intends for our world. In a world clamoring for bigger walls, God invites us to enlarge our tables and make space for the other—whoever that happens to be in our context.

In all of these ways, those who struggle with the exclusive claims of many worldviews, especially on the basis of how those beliefs have been used to justify all kinds of evil, will find an advocate in the person of Jesus. To follow in the way of Jesus is to tread a difficult but life-giving path that insists that Jesus is still the way, the truth, and the life, and yet refuses to marginalize people or act in disrespectful ways toward their cherished beliefs.

The way of Jesus is the way of radical self-sacrificing love that should prompt you to invite different people into your life. Welcome them to your table to listen, to learn, to share, to discuss, and even to debate, communicating with your posture and your presence a love that goes far beyond ideological agreement or shared religious beliefs.

Part 3

Building a Positive Case

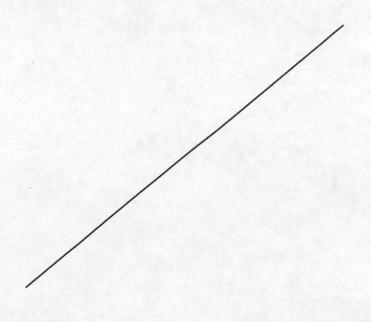

7. The Reasonableness of Belief in God

ANDY STEIGER

My 1987 Jeep Wrangler and a couple of boxes in the back seat were all my earthly belongings the day I left home for college. Packing up my childhood possessions marked an important transition into adulthood; I spent most of that day deliberating over which memorabilia would be stored in the garage and which would come with me. Not much made the cut! At the end of the day, my mom and stepdad came out onto the driveway to see me off. With tears in her eyes, my mom gave me a big hug and a kiss and wished me well on my journey. It was difficult to leave, but exciting at the same time. I shut my car door, gave a quick wave, and was off to face the world.

In time, I began to appreciate that it was much more than just my belongings I was picking through that day as I left for college—it was also my beliefs. Leaving home begins a process in which we deliberate over the beliefs we have collected in our youth and begin to determine which ones will get left behind and which will come along with us. It's a journey that we all embark on as we develop our worldview.

A worldview is like a pair of glasses that affects how each person uniquely sees the world. It encompasses all of our assumptions and beliefs, from the most mundane to the most profound: from our feelings about chocolate milkshakes to our understanding of gravity, politics, or education. Whether we are aware of

> What we need to ask is not whether we have a worldview, but rather how closely our current worldview resembles reality.

it or not, we all have a distinct view of the world pieced together from our experiences and the facts we gather along the way. What we need to ask, then, is not whether we have a worldview, but rather how closely our current worldview resembles reality. Do we have sound evidence for our beliefs about life? Or, as the ancient Greek thinker

Plato, who lived about 423–348 BC, put it: is what we believe true, good, and beautiful?[1]

PACKED UP BELIEFS

When I arrived at college, it didn't take long for me to realize that not all my beliefs about the world were true or good—and they were definitely not all beautiful! This became clear to me four months into college life when a purplish substance suddenly appeared in my toilet. I confronted my three roommates with whom I shared a bathroom. I thought that maybe someone had spilled paint in the toilet bowl and not bothered to clean it up. Through their laughter, my roommates explained to me, with a sense of pride, that together we had been growing mold! I was appalled. I had no idea that a toilet had to be cleaned; my worldview just assumed that toilets were self-cleaning. It was equally disturbing to discover that there are people in this world who would enjoy growing mold in their toilet. I promptly cleaned it.

I had not previously appreciated all that my mom had done for me growing up, but now my worldview was expanding for the better. In college, I began to re-think all of my beliefs, from the small to the large, and because of this I was beginning to see the world differently.

One of the views of the world that I had inherited growing up concerned God. Shortly before my parents separated, my mom had become a Christian. Her relationship with God not only brought her life meaning, but it also became her source of beauty and strength; it had a way of infusing her with passion for life and a love for other people. As I was growing up, I watched my mom's relationship with God and that helped form my own Christian worldview.

However, when I moved away from home and went to college, I was confronted with the reality of my beliefs. No one was dragging me to church. I no longer needed to pray before meals. These were now my choices. How would I live? We are all eventually faced with a time when we realize that what we believe about the world has a direct impact on the way we live in it. So, one day I confronted myself on the inconsistencies of my beliefs and actions. "Andy," I said, "Do you really believe that God exists? I mean *really* believe it?" It was a life-changing question.

THE PROBLEM OF FINDING
ABSOLUTE CERTAINTY

The vast majority of the world's population believes that a God exists.[2] It's a belief that seems to come naturally to humankind. Research even indicates that this is true of children; we're born with a bent toward believing in a God or gods.[3] But that doesn't mean it's true. After all, I initially believed that toilets cleaned themselves, and that certainly wasn't true! Likewise, while I was attracted to God because of how I saw him reflected in my mother's life, that alone didn't prove the existence of God. It merely provided evidence for the therapeutic effect of *believing in* a God. I also see God poorly reflected in people's lives, but again, what does that prove? It might help prove the fickleness of people, but certainly not the nonexistence of God. How then can we determine if God does or does not exist? Can his existence be proven with absolute certainty?

The problem is that there are few things, if any, that we can prove with that kind of certainty. Asking for absolute certainty is setting the bar too high. We don't have 100 percent proof for any of our most basic and cherished beliefs.

Consider the 1999 movie *The Matrix*. In the movie, the "reality" all humans perceive with their five senses is really just an elaborate computer simulation called the Matrix, which was set up and maintained by sentient machines that had rebelled against humankind.

> Asking for absolute certainty is setting the bar too high.

The humans living in the Matrix are unaware that they are in a simulation, and it's only by taking a red pill that they "wake up" and realize the truth about the world.

As frightening as it is, this scenario is not a new one. While *The Matrix* popularized it, the concept of humans being unaware of true reality has been intriguing philosophers for centuries. Plato wondered if perhaps human reality is like being stuck in a cave and watching shadows dance on the wall, with the true reality happening just outside of our perception.[4] The French philosopher René Descartes (1596–1650) suggested that there could be an evil demon who has deluded all of our senses, making us think that we have a body and that there is an external world, when in reality there is neither.[5] More recently, Swedish philosopher Nick Bostrom has come up with the "simulation argument," in which he attempts to mathematically predict the likelihood that our reality is actually a computer simulation set up by more advanced civilizations.[6]

Why do these people keep going on about something that seems obviously false to the rest of us? Of course we don't live in a computer simulation! The problem is that we can't really prove it. Not 100 percent. To that level of certainty, we can't prove that we exist, that our senses are trustworthy, that our capacity for reason is dependable, or any of our other most basic beliefs. Perhaps the most certain we can be about anything is summarized in Descartes's famous axiom, "I think, therefore I am."[7] Basically, it means that if there is one thing that I can surely be confident of, it is that I am thinking, and if I am thinking, then I must exist. After all, the very act of doubting your own existence would prove that you have a mind, and therefore, that you do exist. Beyond that, proving anything in this world 100 percent is nearly impossible.

BEYOND A REASONABLE DOUBT

If proving anything 100 percent is so difficult, why do we demand that level of certainty for the existence of God? Instead, it's far more realistic to look for evidence that demonstrates God's existence is *reasonable*. After all, this is how we determine all of the rest of our beliefs. Even though I can't prove 100 percent that I can trust my senses and I don't live in the Matrix, I have good reasons to believe that I don't.

This is how our justice system works. In a criminal investigation, there are many cases in which there is no *absolute* certainty of "whodunit," only degrees of likelihood on which a case is built and a jury deliberates. After all, even if a suspect confesses to the crime, there is always the possibility, however remote, that they are lying. Therefore, the standard of the jury's judgment in a criminal conviction is "beyond all *reasonable* doubt." This is how all of our beliefs are developed, including the belief that God exists.

> It's far more realistic to look for evidence that demonstrates God's existence is *reasonable*.

I'm not saying that you can't be absolutely confident in your belief in God. I believe you can. I just don't believe that you can *prove* that belief with absolute certainty, nor do I believe you need to in order for belief in God to be justified.

When we ask, "Does God exist?" we are seeking to examine the evidence and determine in which direction the scales are tipping, be it ever so slightly or significantly in favor of God's existence or not. Tipping our personal scales becomes a verdict for belief. Like a scale, the more evidence we

> Faith can be defined as trusting what you have good reason to believe is true.

accumulate, the weightier our convictions grow. This is why, according to the Christian worldview, faith can be defined as trusting what you have good reason to believe is true.

So, what amounts to good reason? Let's turn now to the telescope and the microscope and examine some evidence for God.

EVIDENCE FROM THE TELESCOPE

I remember clearly the first time I looked through a telescope. When I was in middle school, I had a good friend whose father was an amateur astronomer. They lived far enough away from the city to be free from light pollution and, one evening, they set the telescope up on the front lawn. I climbed up on a little stool, peered into the lens, and there it was: Saturn! It was 1.2 billion kilometers away and we could see it clear as day—even the rings. It was awe-inspiring. A few minutes later, my friend's father swung the telescope around and aimed it at the Milky Way, a hazy streak of light in the sky—it was all stars! I had no idea that the Milky Way was made up of billions of stars!

Besides the sun, the closest star to earth is Proxima Centauri. If we traveled at the speed of light, it would take over four years to get there. That's unbelievably far; yet, to travel completely across our Milky Way Galaxy would take over 100,000 light years.[8] That's unfathomable to me! Yet, if that's how big our galaxy is, what about the size of the entire universe?

Modern astronomy has revealed a complex and immense universe that defies human comprehension. Have you ever wondered just how big the universe is? Well, some astronomers decided to do an experiment to find out.[9] They pointed the Hubble Space Telescope toward a small square section of space and started taking pictures. They returned regularly over the next ten years until they had over 2,000 images. What did they find? In that small square of space, they counted over 5,500 new galaxies that had never been seen before, each of which contained billions of stars! In total, scientists now estimate that the observable universe contains 100–200 billion galaxies—and that's just the *observable* universe! They are convinced there is more out there that we just can't see. Meanwhile, here we sit: in a small galaxy, on a tiny blue rock, orbiting a massive burning star. Shouldn't we all be amazed that we find ourselves in such a predicament? I mean, have you ever considered where all this came from and how we got here?

A Roman Catholic priest and scientist named Georges Lemaître (1894–1966) thought long and hard about this question. In 1927, he became the first to propose the theory of an expanding universe, a theory that would later be adopted widely among scientists and called the *Big Bang theory*. Essentially, this theory holds that the universe began as an infinitely dense singularity, a starting point, which exploded, has been expanding ever since, and will continue to expand until all of its energy is expelled. This was a huge development that made the questions of our origin even more amazing. Until this point, scientists had believed that the universe was eternal, an idea we inherited from Aristotle. Now, scientists were seeing that the universe had a beginning and an end. Naturally, the question arose: What or who is responsible?

The kalam cosmological argument, popularized by William Lane Craig, puts the problem of the origin of the universe like this:

1. Whatever begins to exist has a cause.

2. The universe began to exist.

3. Therefore, the universe has a cause.

Just like a crime scene, whenever there's an explosion, we study the evidence to deduce what the cause was. Some people believe the physical universe is all that exists (closed universe), while others believe that there could be something that exists beyond the physical (open universe). Now think for a moment. If the physical universe is all that exists, then what was there before the physical universe came into existence?

There was nothing.

Well then, what caused the universe to come into existence? Nothing? Some people suggest that the universe caused itself, that it came from nothing, by nothing, and for nothing.[10] Logic, however, tells us that from nothing you get ... nothing!

Christianity refers to the explosion of the universe into existence as creation *ex nihilo*, "from nothing." However, this doesn't mean that the universe came from nothing, but rather that it came from nothing physical.

In that case, what created the universe? Genesis 1:1 tells us that "in the beginning God created the heavens and the earth." The Christian worldview proposes that before the universe came into being, there was nothing physical. Instead, there was something non-physical and eternal—God.

Often I hear people object to this conclusion, asking, "Okay then, who created God?" It's important not to draw a false comparison. Notice that the universe must have had a cause because it had a beginning; it came *into* existence. God, on the other hand, does not have a birthdate; he did not come into existence, and so no cause is required. As the first premise of the kalam cosmological argument says, only what *begins* to exist needs a cause.

> The Christian worldview proposes that before the universe came into being, there was nothing physical. Instead, there was something non-physical and eternal—God.

Now some people may claim that God being eternal is absurd or counts as special pleading.[11] Yet consider that up until a hundred years ago, the dominant worldview held that the universe was eternal. Nobody seemed to have a problem with that view until the evidence demonstrated otherwise.

More and more I hear people pointing toward quantum mechanics as a possible explanation for how you can get something from nothing. Granted, we do see some incredible things at the quantum level, but what we have never seen is creation from nothing. William Lane Craig explains the problem with this view:

> The quantum vacuum is not what most people envision when they think of a vacuum—that is, absolutely nothing. On the contrary, it's a sea of fluctuating energy, an arena of violent activity that has a rich physical structure and can be described by physical laws. ... We have to ask, well, what is the origin of the whole quantum vacuum itself? Where does it come from? ... You've simply pushed back the issue of creation. Now you've got to account for how this very active ocean of fluctuating energy came into being.[12]

It is true that quantum fluctuations can occur with seemingly no cause whatsoever. However, that's not the point of this argument. The premise is that whatever *begins to exist* has a cause: quantum mechanics came into existence during the Big Bang, therefore it can't be the cause. Something can't bring itself into existence. This is the problem with all of science's attempted solutions to the problem of creation from nothing, from the oscillating model to the multiverse. Like it or not, eventually there needs to be an eternal, uncaused cause, something that has the attributes of God. Otherwise, you end up with an infinite regress of causes—you begin the absurd, never-ending inquiry of asking, "What caused *that*? OK, what caused *that*?" Therefore, there is good reason to conclude that God is the foundation from which everything else came.

> Eventually there needs to be an eternal, uncaused cause, something that has the attributes of God.

WHO IS THIS FIRST CAUSE?

Like a crime scene, the more I peer through the telescope, the more I find myself asking, "Who did it?" William Lane Craig concludes from the evidence cited above that there is a "necessary, uncaused, timeless, spaceless, immaterial personal Creator of the universe."[13] The first time I heard this, I was surprised. It seemed clear that the evidence was pointing to a creator, but how do we know that the creator is personal or relational and not an impersonal force?

When it comes to non-physical causes, there are only two potential options: the impersonal (an abstract object like the laws of mathematics) or personal (such as an unembodied mind). But there is really only one option since abstract objects, like laws, can't actually cause things. As mathematician John Lennox put it, "In the world in which most of us live, the simple law of arithmetic, $1 + 1 = 2$, never brought anything into being by itself. It certainly has never put any money into my bank account."[14] Therefore, the cause must be personal. The only thing we know of that is both non-physical and capable of causing anything as a first cause is a person; only personal beings are capable of having wills that can act on the universe.

This is what Christianity has always said about God. The Bible asserts that the natural world reveals not only the existence of God but his personal character as well. Romans 1:19–20 says that "what may be known about God is plain to them, because God has made it plain to them. For since the creation of the world God's invisible qualities—his eternal power and divine nature—have been clearly seen, being understood from what has been made." The apostle Paul, who wrote those words, confirmed that the God who made the universe is the same personal God who loves us.

The universe we live in is truly amazing. You might even refer to it as a miracle. Yet there is a miracle even greater than existence, and that's to know that you exist. Albert Einstein put it like this: "The most incomprehensible thing about the universe is that it is comprehensible."[15] It's amazing to think that we are not only aware of our existence but that we can also study the world and understand it. It's not beyond us. Peering into the night sky with a telescope brings us to something personal and relational in nature—a God we can comprehend.

> There is a miracle even greater than existence, and that's to know that you exist.

EVIDENCE FROM THE MICROSCOPE

Now I want to turn our attention from the grand to the minuscule to see what our existence can tell us about God. Peering through a microscope opens our minds to a whole other world. The universe isn't only immeasurably big—it's also extremely small. In fact, it's difficult to believe, but the world is nearly as small as it is large. Whether you look out or in, the universe will astonish you.

The intricacies of life at the smallest level have always amazed me. This fascination with biology only grew stronger one day in high school biology class when I was greeted by the unpleasant odor of formaldehyde. As I took my seat, a dead frog awaited my scalpel. The art of dissection reminded me of being a kid; when I was younger, I had the habit of taking things apart all around our house, only to realize that I could never put them back together again. My poor mother nearly went mad from my destructive curiosity. As I took apart that frog, I was both disturbed and awestruck. Clearly, this was much more complex than taking apart a toaster!

The curiosity of scientific discovery has always led biologists to "disassemble" human life, and advances in the last century have allowed them to do this down to the molecular level. In the process, they discovered a world of unfathomable complexity. For a long time, we have known about our organs and tissues, but the advancement of the microscope has revealed the further details of cells, proteins, and amino acids.

The basic components for all living things, from the gigantic to the minuscule, are amino acids. These are the "nuts and bolts" that, when arranged or sequenced correctly, make up proteins. Proteins, in turn, make up the parts of a living cell. Cells comprise tissue; tissues form organs; and organs function together to form an organism, such as a human.

There are around twenty different amino acids found in life.[16] In order to form a protein, 150–3,000 amino acids must be ordered into the correct sequence. Then, between 250–3,000 proteins must be organized in order to form a living cell—the very simplest form of life on earth. Humans are incredibly complex and information-rich, even at our most basic level.

What allows all of those amino acids to get sequenced correctly to create proteins is DNA (deoxyribonucleic acid). DNA comes in long strings that contain all the information needed to make proteins, like a blueprint showing how to construct a person. The Human Genome Project, led by Christian scientist Francis Collins, was the world's largest biological project. It was responsible for mapping the human genome contained within DNA. The scope of this project was immense. Human DNA contains a code that is over three billion letters long—and that's just one strand! The diameter of a DNA molecule is only two nanometers, while the average diameter of a human hair is around 100,000 nanometers. It has been calculated that a single teaspoon could hold one strand of DNA from every species that has ever existed and still have room for the information from every book that has ever been written![17] If your DNA were an instruction manual, it would be approximately 1,000,000 pages long, single-spaced in twelve-point font.

Referring to DNA as complex is an understatement, and current scientific discoveries have only revealed a fraction of the information found in that code. As Microsoft founder Bill Gates said, "DNA is like a computer program, but far, far more advanced than any software we've ever created."[18]

Where did the information found in DNA come from? Some scientists insist that a natural, unguided process, such as evolution, is completely responsible for the origin of life.* Yet the problem with that answer is that the very

---

* Some Christians, including Francis Collins, hold to a view called theistic evolution. Though, like all beliefs, it has many varieties, the basic premise is that everything science currently claims about the process of evolution is true, but that evolution has been guided by, and the materials supplied by, God. As Collins says, "Do not fear, there is plenty of divine mystery left. Many people who have considered all the scientific and spiritual evidence still see God's creative and guiding hand

function of evolution is dependent on the existence of an organism with self-replicating DNA; without genetic material, which has the ability to mutate, natural selection grinds to a halt. Therefore, naturalistic evolution simply cannot account for the existence of genetic material in the first place.[†]

Since naturalistic evolution can't account for the origin of life, we have four potential options. First is the idea that aliens seeded life on earth. However, this has many issues. For example, where did the aliens come from? Did they evolve? If so, where did their genetic material come from,

> Naturalistic evolution simply cannot account for the existence of genetic material in the first place.

---

at work. ... For those who believe in God, there are reasons now to be more in awe, not less" (*The Language of God: A Scientist Presents Evidence for Belief* [New York: Free Press, 2006], 106–7). Although there is much debate surrounding the topic, theistic evolution does not fall victim to the pitfalls discussed in this chapter the way that unguided, naturalistic evolution does, seeing as theistic evolution acknowledges the need for divine creative power.

† Thomas Nagel, an atheist philosopher, agrees: "In the present intellectual climate such a possibility is unlikely to be taken seriously, but I would repeat my earlier observation that no viable account, even a purely speculative one, seems to be available of how a system as staggeringly functionally complex and informationally-rich as a self-reproducing cell, controlled by DNA, RNA, or some predecessor, could have arisen by chemical evolution alone from a dead environment. Recognition of the problem is not limited to the defenders of intelligent design." Thomas Nagel, *Mind and Cosmos: Why the Materialist Neo-Darwinian Conception of Nature Is Almost Certainly False* (Oxford: Oxford University Press, 2012), 123.

and how did they evolve to be smarter than us in a shorter amount of time?

Second is that life occurred by sheer chance or luck. However, scientists have calculated that the odds of even a simple protein being sequenced by chance are around 10^{164}; the odds of the simplest of cells, made of around 250 proteins, being constructed by chance are $10^{41,000}$.[19] For perspective, there are 10^{65} atoms in our galaxy! That's mathematically impossible. There's not enough time or opportunity in the universe for chance to account for the simplest cell, let alone for a human being.

Third, it could be argued that the universe was determined to exist exactly as we see and couldn't be any other way. However, if this was true, we could never know that. If our universe was determined for life, so were all of our beliefs. Thus, if you believe in God, that was determined; if you don't believe in God, that was also determined. Who is right? Who knows! Accordingly, whatever we believe to be true, we would believe *not* because it's true but because we were determined to believe it.

The fourth option is that life was created. The only thing we know that is able to create is a person. God is a person that has the ability and will to create the universe and life.

Skeptics such as Richard Dawkins admit that the immense complexity of life, as found in DNA, make it appear designed, but they continue to assert that this is in appearance only.[20] But why believe that? After all, the simplest and most intuitive answer is that DNA looks designed because it *is* designed.

The biological complexity of DNA is a part of the incredible cumulative evidence pointing toward an author of life. At the same time, it also points to much more than that. Although my DNA is coded for life, my life is not fully coded. I am more than DNA; I am a person, with a unique mind and the freedom to love, believe, and hope. I am free to make choices, even the decision of whether I believe God exists. It's incredible! I have the capacity to weigh the evidence from the telescope and microscope and decide for myself if the cosmos and myself are a meaningless cosmic explosion or the purposeful creation of God. More than that, I have the capacity to know and be known, to love and be loved.[21]

CONCLUSION

During my time at college and since, I have worked through many of my beliefs and doubts. I have firmly reached the conclusion that the universe only makes sense through the lens of a Christian worldview. As C. S. Lewis, a former atheist, declared, "I believe in Christianity as I believe that the sun has risen: not only because I see it, but because by it I see everything else."[22]

I can't prove with absolute certainty that God exists or that he loves me, but as we have seen, that kind of proof is extremely hard to come by in any area of life. Instead, I have concluded that I have good reason to believe. My confidence in that belief has grown these many years since I first placed my trust in God and said yes to his offer of relationship through Jesus. My relationship with God has changed my worldview, just like it changed my mom's. I not only see the world differently, but I also act differently in it.

Belief in God isn't just intellectual assent; it involves a personal commitment. The best way I can describe it is with an example from my first wedding anniversary. My wife and I celebrated our first year of marriage by throwing ourselves out of a plane (which, oddly enough, is a similar experience to getting married!). Before I plunged 10,000 feet to the earth with my beautiful wife, I had good reasons to trust my parachute: I had taken physics in high school. I understood how velocity and drag worked. I knew the facts. I even had eyewitness testimonies that said it worked. Yet in the end, to truly know whether the parachute worked, I still needed to jump out of that plane—which I did, with some rather high-pitched screaming. Asking my wife, Nancy, to marry me was a similar experience, albeit without the screaming. How did I know she loved me? I couldn't prove that she did, but I did have good reason to believe it.

Faith in God, according to Christianity, is no different. We can study the facts, of which there are many.* Yet aside from facts, Jesus explains that we can also personally experience God. If you haven't yet begun to follow Jesus, what's holding you back? It would seem that you have nothing to lose and everything to gain.

I don't want to give the impression that following God is easy, but neither is jumping from a perfectly good airplane or getting married. It's difficult, and it's normal for there to be times of doubt, fear, and frustration. But in

---

* In this chapter, I have talked about the cosmological argument and the argument from consciousness, but there are also the teleological, ontological, moral, and fine-tuning arguments, to name a few. The next chapter presents a version of the teleological argument.

moments of doubt, I encourage you to go back to the facts. Remind yourself of how you came to your belief. Most of all, I encourage you to place your trust in God. Seek to know God—he wants to know you! After all, he created you to be with him.

8. How Fine-Tuning Points Powerfully to God

MICHAEL HORNER

ave you ever heard anyone assert there is no evidence for the existence of God? You will if you haven't already. The most vocal atheists repeatedly say this. I find it difficult to understand, though, how anyone can be so dismissive of the quantity and quality of evidence that there is for God's existence.

After forty years of researching, writing, speaking, and debating on this topic, I think it can be shown that God's existence is considerably more probable than not. Despite the confident assertions of many atheists to the contrary, my considered opinion is that there are good arguments that provide a reasonably strong cumulative case for the existence of God.

In this chapter, I will look at one such argument, sometimes called the "teleological argument" or the "fine-tuning argument." It is built on a remarkable scientific discovery that points powerfully to an intelligent mind behind the universe. So what exactly is this "fine-tuning," and how could it serve as a pointer to God?

WHAT IS FINE-TUNING?

As early as the 1970s, scientists have been astonished to find that our universe appears balanced on a razor's edge for the existence of life. Like the little bear's porridge in the story of "Goldilocks and the Three Bears," the constants in the laws of nature and the initial quantities of the "stuff" in the universe are "just right" for life to exist! Tiny changes in any one of these values would have destroyed the possibility of life of any kind anywhere in the cosmos, and in most cases they would have destroyed the cosmos itself. Astrophysicist Luke Barnes explains:

> Scientists have been astonished to find that our universe appears balanced on a razor's edge for the existence of life.

> A universe that has just small tweaks in the fundamental constants might not have any of the chemical bonds that give us molecules, so say farewell to

DNA, and also to rocks, water, and planets. Other tweaks could make the formation of stars or even atoms impossible. And with some values for the physical constants, the universe would've flickered out of existence in a fraction of a second. That the constants are all arranged in what is, mathematically speaking, the very improbable combination that makes our grand, complex, life bearing universe possible is what physicists mean when they talk about the "fine-tuning" of the universe for life.[1]

In other words, as Sir Martin Rees, Britain's Astronomer Royal, has declared, "Wherever physicists look, they see examples of fine-tuning."[2]

One specific example of fine-tuning is the gravitational constant, which determines the strength of gravity in our universe. Imagine a dial divided into 10^{60} (10 followed by 60 zeros) equal units that represent all the possible values that the gravitational constant could have taken. To put this number into context, note that the number of cells in your body is 10^{14}, the number of seconds that have passed since the beginning of time is 10^{20}, and the number of protons in the entire universe is 10^{80}! The accuracy required for one part in 10^{60} is comparable to hitting a one-square-inch target on the other side of the observable universe with one shot. Now, I was a pretty accurate three-point shooter in my basketball playing days, but accuracy like this is ridiculously beyond anything conceivable for me, Steph Curry, or the world's greatest military sniper.

If the dial was tweaked by merely one of these infinitesimally small units, the force of gravity would be very different and none of us would be here. That tiny adjustment in either direction would produce a universe that either expands rapidly and disperses into a thin soup or collapses very quickly back upon itself in a big crunch. In either case there would be no stars, no planets, no life!

To give another example, picture another dial representing all the possible values the cosmological constant could take. (The cosmological constant is a kind of anti-gravity repulsive force that determines the expansion rate of the universe.) A minuscule alteration on this dial by only one part in 10^{120} would also have produced a universe expanding too rapidly for galaxies, stars, and planets to form or a universe collapsing back on itself—life-prohibiting universes either way!

And there are many more dials that could be mentioned. If the weak force found in atoms had been different by only one part in 10^{100}, again the universe would not be life-permitting. If the strong nuclear force—the glue that holds protons and neutrons together in the nuclei of atoms—was slightly weaker, nuclei would not be stable and the periodic table would disappear. If it was set slightly stronger, the intense heat of the early universe would have converted all hydrogen into helium, and there would be no such thing as water! This would also mean that "99.97 percent of the 24 million carbon compounds we have discovered would be impossible."[3] Again, no life!

One final incredible example of fine-tuning is the entropy of the early universe. The second law of thermodynamics says that the entropy of an isolated system always increases—in other words, it is prone to greater and greater disorder. A Big Bang should have produced a universe with virtually zero order (high entropy), and yet our universe came out very orderly. The entropy of the early universe was astonishingly low! Oxford physicist Roger Penrose calculates the odds of the special low-entropy condition of our universe having arisen by sheer chance as being at least as small as one part in 10^{10} [123]. Penrose says, "I cannot even recall seeing anything else in physics whose accuracy is known to approach, even remotely, a figure like" that one.[4] This is how incredibly narrow the range is for any kind of life to be able to exist in our universe.

POSSIBLE EXPLANATIONS
FOR FINE-TUNING

The fine-tuning of the universe is a scientific fact that requires an explanation, an answer to the question, "Why is the universe like this?" There are only three options: physical necessity, chance, or design. Let's examine these three options, beginning with physical necessity.

Physical necessity means that the values of the constants and quantities of our universe could not have been other than what they are. That is, the universe must permit life. Or to say it another way, life-prohibiting universes would be physically impossible.

The problem with this view is that it is unaccompanied by any proof. There is no reason why the constants or quantities couldn't be different. After all, the laws of nature do not determine the constants or quantities found in the initial conditions. Both are independent of the laws of nature. In fact, superstring theory permits 10^{500} versions of space-time, with the same laws of nature but with varying values for the constants—and nearly all of these possible universes are life-prohibiting.[5]

> The fine-tuning of the universe is a scientific fact that requires an explanation, an answer to the question, "Why is the universe like this?"

Even atheists Stephen Hawking and Leonard Mlodinow, in their book *The Grand Design,* do not accept physical necessity: "It appears that the fundamental numbers, and even the form, of the apparent laws of nature are not demanded by logic or physical principle."[6] Physicist Paul Davies, likewise, claims: "It seems ... that the physical universe does not have to be the way it is: it could have been otherwise."[7]

Physical necessity, therefore, doesn't seem to be warranted by the facts. The constants and quantities are not determined by physics. So if the values of the constants and quantities didn't have to be the way they are, did we just get unbelievably lucky and win the cosmic lottery?

This brings us to *chance,* the second possible explanation for fine-tuning. Sometimes improbable things do happen. But can chance explain the fine-tuning of our universe? This is a more common proposed explanation for fine-tuning, so I'll spend more time looking at it.

FREE THROWS AND FINE-TUNING

To give you an idea of the odds of a universe being fine-tuned by chance, imagine someone shooting a hundred basketball free throws in a row at one time and place. Would you bet a substantial amount of your money on someone who claims he could make all of them? One day I set out to accomplish just such a feat. With my best friend there to rebound and keep count, I sank eighty-nine in a row, but then I missed one. I sank the next ten and called it a day. I have offered a $100 prize to the players I have coached over the last twenty-five years to beat my record. No one has ever come close, and I have coached some very good shooters, including my two sons. I am hoping one of my current players might do it this season. It is clearly not impossible to sink a hundred in a row. I almost did it!

But what about trying to sink 10^{120} free throws in a row? Would you bet your life savings that someone is able to do that? Of course not! Numbers like that are just too ridiculously improbable. It is not reasonable to accept those odds. Yet Leonard Susskind, a professor of theoretical physics at Stanford, and philosopher Robert Kuhn agree that the odds of accidental chance being behind our fine-tuned universe is exactly this: 1 out of 10^{120}.[8]

Chance isn't a reasonable explanation for the finely tuned data because life-prohibiting universes are incomprehensibly more probable than any kind of life-permitting universes. The probability that all the constants and quantities of our universe would, by chance alone, fall into the life-permitting range is so tiny as to be virtually nil!

At a Canadian Royal Society conference I attended in 1985, I remember listening to objections to the fine-tuning argument like "improbable things happen all the time." After all, it is improbable that anyone wins the lottery when they do. And "this universe is just as unlikely as any other universe." Just like any one deal of the cards is as unlikely as any other deal of the cards, so too there is no difference in the probability of any single universe.

> Chance isn't a reasonable explanation for the finely tuned data because life-prohibiting universes are incomprehensibly more probable than any kind of life-permitting universes.

Right away I knew there was a kernel of truth in these statements, but I also knew that something was not quite right with how they were being applied to the fine-tuning argument. Starting with some doodling at that conference, I have worked over the years on some analogies that I think can expose what is mistaken about these objections. Here is one of them.*

ROYAL FLUSHES AND FINELY TUNED UNIVERSES

If you and I are playing high stakes poker and I consistently get dealt a royal flush while you get dealt a weaker hand, how long would it take before you get suspicious? Once, twice, three times? If, when you accuse me of cheating, I respond, "Chill out, dude! The improbable happens all the time, you know," would you accept that explanation? More importantly, how long are you going to keep playing poker with me?

If you know that you would have accused me of cheating at cards pretty early on in my example, and stopped playing, then this shows that you really don't buy the objection that "improbable things happen all the time" or "any one deal of the cards is as unlikely as any other

---

* Many others have come up with similar examples. See Lewis and Barnes, *A Fortunate Universe*, 250–53.

deal of the cards" in the poker game. And you shouldn't buy it either as an explanation for the fine-tuning of the universe.

Yes, the probability of any one deal of five cards compared to any other one deal is equal, but when further specifications are made, the odds change. While it's true that "any one deal of the cards is as unlikely as any one other deal of the cards," the odds of getting a royal flush on one deal are much smaller than getting any of the non-royal flush combinations of five cards. The chances of drawing any royal flush (there are four possible types corresponding to the four different suits—spades, hearts, diamonds, and clubs) is 1 out of 649,739. But add more specification and the odds of drawing a royal flush of spades, for example, is much less—1 out of 2,598,959!

In the same way, "every universe is as unlikely as any other universe." However, the odds of getting a universe that is finely tuned for life is considerably less than getting a life-prohibiting universe. Any two particular universes might be equally improbable, but the number of possible universes that are life-prohibiting far outnumber the number of possible universes that are life-permitting. That means the odds that our universe would be life-permitting are much lower than the odds it would be life-prohibiting. And the numbers we looked at earlier overwhelm us with just how much less so.

So the first problem with chance as an explanation is that it starts by comparing our universe to any other single universe. But we are not asking what the probability of one universe is compared to any other single universe. Rather, we are asking what the probability is of one specified universe (life-permitting) compared to all the other universes lacking that specification (life-prohibiting).

There is a second problem with the chance explanation. It is assuming the cards and universes are being generated randomly, but that is an illegitimate assumption.* Whether the cards or universes are being generated randomly or not is precisely the question at hand. In their excellent book *A Fortunate Universe: Life in a Finely Tuned Cosmos*, astrophysicists Geraint Lewis and Luke Barnes accurately capture what was behind my intuitive skepticism to the chance explanation:

> What matters is not the probability of this Universe compared to the probability of some other universe.

---

* This amounts to begging the question against the fine-tuning argument and the design conclusion, which is fallacious reasoning.

Rather, we should be considering the probability of this Universe given different theories about how this Universe came to be this way.[9]

When we assume that I am dealing the cards fairly, the only conclusion we can draw is that a wildly improbable event must have happened. But we are missing the point that there is another available explanation that is way more probable: I am not dealing the cards fairly. In other words, what may be behind the suspicious dealing is our third possible explanation for a fine-tuned universe: design.

Just as we should be comparing the probability of numerous royal flushes being dealt by random chance or by design (cheating), we should also be comparing the odds of this universe, with its fine-tuning, coming into existence by random chance or design. In both cases, the odds overwhelmingly favor design.

In addition, given that in poker a royal flush cannot be beaten, it is much more likely to be dealt by a cheater than by a fair player. On the other hand, the weak hands you get dealt in our imagined poker game provide no particular advantage, and so are about as likely to be dealt by a fair dealer as by a cheater. It is the difference between these probabilities that imply I am cheating, even if you don't know how.

Applying this to fine-tuning, the statement "this universe is as improbable as any other universe" is only true if we assume that the parameters of our universe are generated randomly. But this is precisely the idea that proponents of the fine-tuning argument are questioning, just as you are rightly questioning my "random" dealing of the cards.

Just as we should be comparing the probability of numerous royal flushes being dealt by random chance or by design (cheating), we should also be comparing the odds of this universe, with its fine-tuning, coming into existence by random chance or design.

Just as we should consider alternative explanations for the royal flushes, like cheating, we should also consider alternative explanations, like design, for the fine-tuning of our universe. Given that only finely tuned universes can support life, it is much more likely that a finely tuned universe is produced by a designer. On the other hand, life-prohibiting universes provide no advantage for life and so are about as likely to be produced by random chance as by a designer.[10]

THE MANY-WORLDS HYPOTHESIS

Given the odds, chance is not really a viable explanatory option for fine-tuning, so those who want to stick with blind luck as an explanation have been forced to extreme speculations that go beyond observable, empirical science to keep chance alive—the multiverse. The multiverse, or *many-worlds hypothesis*, is the view that the existence of a finely tuned universe like ours is bound to happen entirely by chance if there are an infinite number of universes, each with a randomly generated set of constants and quantities. Eventually, a finely tuned universe is going to appear entirely by chance.

But should we believe in it? There are good reasons for being skeptical of the multiverse. First, there just is no evidence for the existence of the multiverse. More importantly, there never could be any evidence. As Lewis and Barnes make clear, the multiverse "cannot be directly detected. If the multiverse exists, we will never get information from the other universes. They could all disappear tomorrow and we'd never know."[11]

Second, the multiverse requires a universe generator that produces an infinite number of universes. But there is no empirical evidence for such a mechanism. The hypotheses proposed for spawning these many universes are nothing but conjectures.[12] Moreover, for the multiverse to be an adequate explanation for fine-tuning, it requires that this mechanism itself doesn't require fine-tuning.

> The multiverse gets rid of the cosmic designer only if there is no fine-tuning required for the multiverse.

The multiverse gets rid of the cosmic designer only if there is no fine-tuning required for the multiverse. Luke Barnes summarizes these problems for the multiverse:

> The main selling point for multiverse theory—all those other universes with different fundamental constants—will forever remain beyond observational confirmation. And even if we postulate a multiverse, we would still need a more fundamental theory to explain how all these universes are generated, which could raise all the same kinds of fine-tuning problems.[13]

Astrophysicist George Ellis of the University of Cape Town is one of the most knowledgeable people about cosmology in the world today. When asked in a *Scientific American* article whether he was a fan of multiverse theories, he responded that they were "unproveable" and involved "much too much untestable speculation about existence of infinities of entities, ill defined and untestable probability measures."[14]

Craig summarizes, "With the failure of the Many Worlds Hypothesis, the alternative of chance collapses. Neither physical necessity nor chance provides a good explanation of the fine-tuning of the universe."[15] The most likely explanation for the fine-tuning of our universe continues to be that it was designed to be that way.

TWO OBJECTIONS

I have been defending the fine-tuning argument on university campuses around the world for nearly four decades, and I have heard a few frequently raised objections. I would like to deal with two of them here.

One objection that is usually raised under the heading of "the anthropic principle" is that you ought not be surprised at the fine-tuning of the universe for life because, after all, if it weren't fine-tuned you wouldn't be here to be surprised about it.

However, numerous thinkers have pointed out that just because the only thing we can observe is a life-permitting universe does not remove the need to explain why a life-permitting universe exists.[16] Given that vanishingly few of the values of the constants and initial conditions of our universe will support intelligent life, how is it that we are here observing and discussing the conditions of our early universe? This is extremely surprising.

Thirty years ago when I was having lunch with philosopher John Leslie, an early expert on the fine-tuning argument, he shared a very helpful analogy in response to this objection. He described a thought experiment of being before a large group of trained marksmen, all with rifles aimed at your heart at point blank range, and you hear the command, "Fire!" You hear all the guns go off and then you notice that you are still alive!

What should you conclude? You shouldn't be surprised that you don't observe that you are dead, because if you were dead, you couldn't observe it! But you should be surprised that you observe that you are alive in view of the improbability of all the marksmen missing. In fact, you should conclude that they all missed on purpose—that it was the result of some kind of a setup, planned by someone for some reason.[17] Even the atheist physicist David Deutsch chides his fellow scientists who dismiss fine-tuning, "If anyone claims not to be surprised by the special features the universe has, he is hiding his head in the sand. These special features are surprising and unlikely."[18]

Another objection to the claim that the universe is fine-tuned for intelligent life is, "If the universe is fine-tuned for life, why is it so large, old, and mostly hostile to life?" This objection misunderstands what "fine-tuning" means. It doesn't mean that life can or should exist everywhere. Philosopher Tim Barnett's response is golden: "To complain about a finely tuned universe not having *more* locations for life misses the point completely. Fine-tuning only tells us that there can be the possibility of life, not that life will be possible *everywhere*."[19]

In addition, many of the "hostile to life" regions of the universe are essential to life elsewhere. Life cannot exist on a star, but stars are vital for life. Exploding stars provide the heavy elements dispersed throughout space that make life possible.[20] We cannot live in the vast vacuum of space, but that does not mean that the vacuum does not play a vital role in making our universe life-permitting and discoverable. If the vacuum of space were filled with breathable air, gravity would cause our universe to collapse almost immediately. Even though space is directly unfriendly to life, indirectly it still plays a necessary role in our life-permitting universe. Lewis and Barnes conclude, "It suffices to say that this Universe is not a waste of space. The vacuum, believe it or not, plays its part in making our Universe life-permitting and discoverable."[21]

The enormous size, age, and emptiness of expanding space are essential for life. It takes a universe billions of light years in size and billions of years old to provide the furnace of stars and supernovae to form and disperse the building blocks of life: carbon, oxygen and nitrogen.*

Clearly, these two additional objections fail to undermine the force of the fine-tuning argument. The explanation that the initial parameters of the universe have been carefully dialed to astonishingly precise amounts in order

---

* Appealing to evolution and the possibility that a different type of life could evolve under different conditions does not undermine fine-tuning either. We are talking about conditions that exist long before there are any life forms that can adapt to an environment. Lewis and Barnes nail the door shut on this objection: "The extremes of parameter space are not just hot and cold. Rather, they are disintegrating atoms, the cessation of all chemical reactions, the crush of a black hole, and the eternal loneliness of life in a universe where particles collide every trillion years or so." Lewis and Barnes, *A Fortunate Universe*, 244.

for life to exist is not only plausible, but reasonable. Given the other options we've studied in this chapter, it seems clear that the best explanation of this fine-tuning is that an intelligent mind designed the universe.

CONCLUSION: A PERSONAL RESPONSE TO A PERSONAL GOD

Physicist and agnostic Paul Davies declares, "There is for me powerful evidence that there is something going on behind it all. ... It seems as though somebody has fine-tuned nature's numbers to make the universe. The impression of design is overwhelming."[22] Philosopher Alvin Plantinga concurs:

> One reaction to these apparent enormous coincidences is to see them as substantiating the theistic claim that the Universe has been created by a personal God and as offering the material for a properly restrained theistic argument—hence the fine-tuning argument. It's as if there are a large number of dials that have to be tuned to within extremely narrow limits for life to be possible in our Universe. It is extremely unlikely that this should

happen by chance, but much more likely that this
should happen, if there is such a person as God.[23]

The fine-tuning argument points us to a transcendent
intelligence behind the universe. Moreover, intelligence is
a function of personhood. Energy does not think—forces
like electricity or electromagnetism are not intelligent.
This scientific discovery of fine-tuning, therefore, also
points to a personal designer of the universe.

Now, acknowledging that the universe is designed is
not the same as believing in the Christian God. When I
am trying to make a case for God's existence, I normally
like to base it on at least three
arguments that I find very per-
suasive. A longer chapter would
have allowed me to consider
another argument based on a
scientific discovery that points powerfully to God—that
the universe had a beginning. This argument, called the
kalam cosmological argument (covered in Andy Steiger's
chapter "The Reasonableness of Belief in God"), points us
to a transcendent cause of space, time, matter, and energy,
and is thus timeless, uncaused, changeless, space-less,

> The fine-tuning
> argument points us
> to a transcendent
> intelligence behind
> the universe.

immaterial, and enormously powerful. From a third argument, the moral argument, it's possible to discover that this transcendent yet personal being's nature is not only perfectly good but is the standard of goodness. This cumulative case points to a being much like the Judeo-Christian God. A rational person who is truly open to the possibility of not only God's existence but a personal relationship with this God should acknowledge that it is at least more probable than not that a being much like the Judeo-Christian God exists.

To make a further case, one would need to look at the historical evidence for Jesus of Nazareth. From studying the life of Jesus and investigating the evidence for his resurrection from the dead three days after he died on a Roman cross (as done in Mark Clark's chapter, "The Hope of the Resurrection"), we would learn that Jesus truly is the incarnation of this God who came to save us from ourselves.

In my experience sharing these arguments with many people over the years, I have noticed some common responses that I find a little unreasonable. Often in a debate my opponent will continue to assert, "There are no good arguments for God's existence," after I've just provided some. Or they will just say "I'm not convinced." Or they will raise some wildly improbable alternative explanation other than God.

It is not enough, though, to respond to arguments for God's existence by just asserting, "There are no good arguments for God's existence." One needs to show which premises in the arguments that we do present are more likely false and why. Mere dislike of the conclusion is insufficient.

Just announcing "I'm not convinced" is also not an adequate response, since this is only a reflection of one's psychological state, not an analysis of the arguments. And there are numerous variables apart from "poor quality of arguments" why one might be "unconvinced."

> Announcing "I'm not convinced" is also not an adequate response, since this is only a reflection of one's psychological state, not an analysis of the arguments.

Finally, claiming or even showing that there is another possible explanation other than God is also not enough to defeat these arguments. One would need to show that the other possibility is more probable than the God hypothesis in each case.

With such a strong case for God, one should consider
if it is possible to know this transcendent yet personal
Creator. My experience and research tell me that this God
loves us and has cleared away the barrier to knowing him
created by our own rebellion. He has done this by Jesus
Christ's death on the cross for us, and he is waiting with
open arms for us to turn to him like modern-day prodigal sons and daughters. He offers us forgiveness and
a new life in a personal relationship with him now and
into eternity, and it is all a free gift that cannot be earned.

9. The Hope of the Resurrection

MARK CLARK

The first time I encountered the idea of death, I was eight years old. We had a cat named Scooter. He got sick. I overheard my parents saying they were going to "put him down." *Put him down?* What was that?

Sounded aggressive.

So I ran out of the cottage where we were staying and into the lake, where I proceeded to dunk my head into the water continuously, attempting to drown myself in protest (which I found out is a difficult way to kill yourself). My family walked out to watch me do this, then slowly got bored and one by one went back inside. After about ten minutes I gave up and came in for dinner. A couple of days later, Scooter was dead.

My second run-in with death was when I was fifteen. My parents had divorced years earlier, and I got a phone call from the hospital one day informing me that my father was dead. He had lung cancer. He was forty-seven. Later, I stood over his casket and asked the big questions of life, but I didn't really have any answers. I hadn't grown up in the church. No Bible. No prayer. No talk of God. My father was such an ardent atheist he made my mother spell my brother's name—Mathew—with one "t" so it wouldn't be biblical.

Four years later, they had me and named me Mark. Clearly, he didn't see the irony. How would he? He had likely never opened a Bible in his life.

Both experiences presented me with the harsh realization that death was final. That's what stung about it. The irreversibility of it all. That is why we cry. That is why we mourn: the finality, the absence of someone who used to be there and now is not. Their seat at the dinner table is no longer occupied. Their side of the bed is empty, with the sheets still pulled up over the pillow. The house is quieter. Their laugh no longer fills the space.

This is where Christianity comes crashing into the finality and the hopelessness of death. Of all the things explored in this book that it offers to us, this may be the most important of all: hope. No, more than that, actually: ultimate hope.

More than any other worldview, Christianity gives us reason to believe that death is not the end. The irreversible reality of death *can* be reversed. Everything sad is "going to come untrue," as Sam Gamgee puts it in Tolkien's *Lord of the Rings*. And the Christian faith proclaims this while never slipping into either sentimentalism—the nonsensical, overemotional reluctance to face the hardships of real life—or the cold, logical arguments for the scholars and academics in their ivory towers. This is why I've come to believe that Christianity is not only the most truthful, but also the most hopeful faith in the marketplace of ideas. The main reason I've come to this conclusion is the resurrection of Jesus Christ from the dead.

AN INVITATION TO INVESTIGATE

As I mentioned, I didn't grow up in a Christian home. I never even walked into a church until I was nineteen years old, and even then I only stayed because there were pretty girls there. The reason I waited to accept Christianity until I was almost in college was that I only like to believe ideas when I have evidence for them. I have always been that way. So, when someone presented Christianity to me in my teen years, I wondered what the evidence was for believing it was true versus other worldview options and religions. Why choose Christianity over the atheism and agnosticism I grew up in, for instance, or the Hindu or Wiccan religions of my friends?

I expected conversations about Christianity to hover around what Jesus taught in comparison to what other religions taught, leaving me with the conclusion that Jesus was the better guy with better ideas about reality, love, and justice. If it worked, all of this would warm my heart and I would become a Christian rather than remain an atheist. But what I was hit with when I began to explore Christianity was that it wasn't primarily a faith about teachings and principles, like other religions. Instead, Christianity was about something that had happened: a historical moment—the crucifixion and resurrection of Jesus. If that event was proven false, the whole thing would fall apart. This intrigued me because it made

Christianity vulnerable to disproof if it was at all made up (like my atheist friends thought), and yet, at the same time, able to be defended through historical evidence if it wasn't a fictitious story.

This makes Christianity utterly unique. Buddhism and Hinduism, for example, are very otherworldly. They are about states of consciousness and enlightenment, and their writings are filled with metaphysical, abstract, spiritual teachings. Judaism and Islam are about the study and practice of law (the Torah and Mishnah, and the Qur'an, respectively). They are about living out an interpretation of authoritative texts and teachings. And while Christianity has aspects of both of these categories (it deals with spiritual realities of the soul, the existence of God, and also reading and following the Bible, which is God's word to humankind), it is only those things if the resurrection is actually true. Amazingly, Christianity doesn't survive if it's only about Jesus' teachings—as good as those are.

> What I was hit with when I began to explore Christianity was that it wasn't primarily a faith about teachings and principles, like other religions. Instead, Christianity was about something that had happened.

You can visit the tombs of the founders of other religions. You can visit the gravesite of Abraham. You can visit the burial place of Muhammad. But you can't do that with Jesus. Well, you can. I did. But the tomb was empty. I spent thousands of dollars, and flew half way around the world, to step into what some people think is the tomb Jesus was buried in, and it was empty!

But it was the most beautiful emptiness. And that's the foundation of Christianity—a historical moment that could potentially be proven false. That's what I loved about it. It is rooted in history. If a person finds the bones of Jesus, Christianity is wrong. Not just not quite accurate, but fully wrong.

If the bones of Jesus get found, shut the lights off and go home because the game is over. Christianity is confident enough in itself to stake the whole thing on a historical event—a miracle nonetheless—that invites historians, scientists, philosophers, and the regular Joe (me and you) to investigate it. So for the rest of this chapter we are going to embark on an investigation of our own. I want to share with you what I discovered when I first took a serious look at Christianity.

THE UNIQUENESS OF
THE RESURRECTION

There are people throughout history who have claimed to see dead people. We tend to chalk these claims up to a few things: either they saw a ghost, ate some bad pizza, or they are altogether delusional. When I started looking at the claim of the resurrection, the question that rose in my mind was, Why did anyone ever *start* believing this about Jesus in the first place? Why did a whole group of people claiming to be eyewitnesses claim that they had seen the resurrected Christ, starting an entire movement in his name with the resurrection as the central claim of their new faith—a claim that they were even willing to die for?

As I started to investigate these questions, it became clear to me that it couldn't be the nature of his death alone. Others have died claiming to be a savior of sorts and it didn't create the same kind of movement as Christianity. In fact, one hundred years on either side of Jesus there were great Jewish teachers who claimed to be the messiah and who started movements, only to be killed by Rome as revolutionaries. Every time, one of two things happened. Either the movement died and everyone went home sad and defeated, or someone else took the leader's place, usually a brother or close cousin, to carry on the movement.

Here is what never happened: no one claimed that their leader was alive again, appearing to his followers, continuing to teach and wanting his followers to continue the mission in his name. That option was never proposed before Christianity. Why is this the case? Why didn't it ever happen before Jesus' followers did it?

On one level, it seems like a natural and obvious step to take: I like my leader. He dies. I just say, "No, he's back from the dead. He showed up at my place and told me stuff. Let's go change the world!" So why didn't that happen before Christianity? The answer is part of the scandal of the Christian story. No one's worldview in the first century would have led them to believe that a single, solitary individual would be raised from the dead in a transformed physical body in the middle of history. Neither the Jews of Jesus' day nor the pagans scattered through the Roman Empire had worldviews that would lead them to expect such a strange occurrence, or even believe it to be possible.

JUDAISM AND PAGANISM

The two major worldviews that were prevalent in the world in which Jesus lived and in which the New Testament was written were Judaism and paganism. In the pagan mind, there was no such thing as resurrection. The Greco-Roman world was influenced by writers like Plato, for whom the spirit world was perfect, pure, right, and filled with beauty, truth, and pleasure. The physical world was seen as fleshly, destructive, and filled with pain, death, and sadness. In the popular Greco-Roman view, the whole point of life was to graduate from this world and enter into a world of disembodied spiritual bliss. In Aeschylus' play *Eumenides*, the god Apollo makes clear that "once a man has died, and the dust has soaked up his blood, there is no resurrection." Resurrection was something that was so looked down on in pagan thought that even in myth it was not permitted. When Apollo tries to bring a child back from death, Zeus punishes him with a thunderbolt.[1] New Testament scholar N. T. Wright summarizes pagan attitudes toward resurrection:

Popular opinion would attempt to bring the dead back if that were possible, but this would be a mistake ... [for death was] seen as something to be desired. ... The reason people do not return ... is that life is so good there; they want to stay, rather than return to the world of space, time and matter.[2]

According to paganism, not only did resurrection not happen, you didn't want it to occur. Judaism had a view on resurrection that was different from paganism, but almost as unlikely to produce the claims of early Christians: for the first-century Jew, resurrection was going to happen at the end of time, and it was going to involve the whole nation of Israel. Judaism in the time of Jesus didn't think in individual terms. Instead, they thought of national movements, which invoked the blessing and

> Jews said resurrection would happen at the end of time and involve the whole nation of Israel, and pagans didn't want it to occur.

cursing of God (Deuteronomy 31–33). And one day, at the end of time, God would judge the world and resurrect Israel to a new world of eternal life and blessing. Everyone else would be resurrected to eternal judgment and punishment (Daniel 12:1–3; Ezekiel 36–37).

In short, Jews said resurrection would happen to a large nation of people at the end of time, and pagans didn't want it to occur. Thus, "Christianity was born into a world where its central claim was known to be false" or unwanted.[3] No one believed in resurrection the way the early Christians did: one man (not the whole nation) resurrected from the dead in the middle of history (not at the end of time). The resurrection of Jesus didn't fit anyone's paradigm. This is one reason why, in the Gospel stories, we find the disciples to be the first skeptics of the resurrection. They arrive at the tomb and their first reaction is to think that someone must have moved or stolen his body (John 20:2, 13). The disciples simply didn't have a category for Jesus' resurrection, which made me start to think that it wasn't something any one would make up, at least not Jews in the first century. And the more I dug into the history, the more evidence I discovered that leaned in this direction.

A SUMMARY OF
THE RELEVANT FACTS

My study of the evidence led me to discover a few well-attested facts surrounding the beginning of

Christianity. First, there was the medical and historical evidence around the death of Jesus by crucifixion. Given the trauma of crucifixion, it became clear to me that the "swoon" theory that Jesus drifted in and out of consciousness while on the cross and then woke up later and appeared to his disciples was unsustainable in light of the medical evidence.

Second, there was the evidence of the missing body. If Jesus had not risen from the dead, his body should have been easy to find given the public location of the tomb—and given how motivated both Rome and the Jewish leadership would have been to find it once the disciples started preaching he rose from the dead.

Third, there was the evidence of the empty tomb, with the grave-clothes left behind, indicating the body wasn't stolen. After all, what type of grave robbers would steal a body and leave the valuable fabric behind? It was nicely folded and set in place, no less.

Fourth, there was the evidence of the post-crucifixion appearances of Jesus (see 1 Corinthians 15:3–9 for a list of eyewitnesses). Hundreds of people, including some skeptics (like James) and hostile unbelievers (like Paul), claimed to witness the resurrected Christ appearing to them, not in a subjective vision, but in a bodily form that could be touched.

None of this evidence by itself may be sufficient to argue convincingly for a resurrection from the dead. But considering all of the data together, I found a sufficient and compelling explanation for the early Christian belief that Jesus really did rise from the dead.[4]

THREE PUSHBACKS

After coming to the conclusion that there was, in fact, good historical evidence for the death and resurrection of Jesus, there were still three major pushbacks that I needed to address before I could truly believe in the resurrection. These are three popular challenges, which I myself believed at one time or another, and which I have now come to see as flawed.

JESUS DIDN'T REALLY DIE.

As with the swoon theory above, some skeptics say one explanation for Jesus' supposed resurrection is that he didn't really die at all. This is actually the official position of Islam.[5] What does one do with this theory?

There are good reasons to treat this explanation with skepticism. First, at least ten writers outside the Bible mention Jesus of Nazareth by name.[6] These were not friends of Christianity, but rather first-century historians—some of them Jewish, some Roman—who were recording history, mostly with an anti-Christian agenda. These writers report a number of different things about Jesus, most making clear that he was killed. For instance, the Jewish historian Josephus writes:

> About this time there lived Jesus, a wise man. ... When Pilate ... condemned him to be crucified, those who had come to love him did not give up their affection for him. On the third day he appeared ... restored to life ... and the tribe of Christians ... has not disappeared. (Josephus, *Antiquities*, 18.63–64)

Second is the way the Romans treated criminals destined for the cross. After all, if there was one thing the Romans knew how to do, it was kill people. Soldiers of Rome would crucify up to six thousand people on a single day, and it is safe to conclude that they did not hammer victims to crosses only to take them down and afterward have them stumble home a few days later. Jesus didn't pass out, wake up a couple hours later, dust himself off, and walk away like he was in a scene from Monty Python. No, the Roman Empire made sure crucified criminals were dead. The idea that the Romans just messed up the crucifixion of Jesus is wishful thinking that does not hold up under serious historical scrutiny.

> The idea that the Romans just messed up the crucifixion of Jesus is wishful thinking that does not hold up under serious historical scrutiny.

THEY WENT TO THE WRONG TOMB.

A second pushback of skeptics is that the women, and later the other disciples, were so distraught in their grief that they showed up at the wrong tomb. They visited the place where they thought the body was laid, but there was never a body there.

Is this likely? I don't think so. I've gotten lost before, as I'm sure you have, too. People make mistakes about where they are going. People even make mistakes about which people have died. The worst mistake I ever made as a pastor was the day I told a woman that her husband was dead and sat grieving with her for forty-five minutes before I realized that I had the wrong guy. I tried to soften the blow by joking with her that the mix-up was kind of a gift, because she got her husband back from the dead—you know, like Jesus. She didn't laugh.

So mistakes happen. But again, let's be honest with the evidence: there is nothing to suggest that this is what happened with Jesus. It's an objection based on nothing. Historians don't buy the wrong tomb theory because those in power could have easily used the dead body of Jesus to stop the early church before it really got going. When rumors of a resurrected hero started, they could have simply rolled out his body. "Look, guys, here is Jesus and he's clearly dead. You just went to the wrong tomb. End of story."

But they didn't do that, because there was no body to be found.

THE STORY WAS AN ELABORATE HOAX.

The New Testament writers intended to record events that actually happened. But why should we trust the New Testament writers? The answer is the resurrection narratives are trustworthy when judged by the critical methods of historical analysis applied by historians to all ancient writings. The criteria historians use when assessing the historical reliability of the events and teachings recorded in the New Testament include the following:

1. Multiple attestations

There are four Gospels and multiple New Testament letters that affirm the resurrection of Jesus actually occurred. This multiple attestation is far more conclusive than one literary record, as is common with other religious texts.

2. Early attestation

There is early evidence for the resurrection of Jesus recorded in 1 Corinthians 15 that is dated by some scholars to within months of the crucifixion and resurrection. Though the first letter to the Corinthians was written more than twenty years after Jesus' death, here the apostle Paul is drawing on a tradition he had been taught by others: "What I received I passed on to you" (1 Corinthians 15:3). This early Christian tradition records Jesus' appearances to early church leaders, including Peter, the twelve disciples, James (Jesus' brother), and more than five hundred people at one time. Many scholars argue that Paul received this tradition from James and Peter when he visited Jerusalem shortly after his own conversion (see Galatians 1:18). The longer the time between an event and the written record of that same event, the more opportunity there is for legendary development to obscure the historical record. But recorded eyewitness testimony this close to the events in question is historical gold and taken with utmost seriousness by modern scholars.

3. Embarrassment

The Gospel writers include content that makes early church leaders look bad. The narratives describing the death and resurrection of Jesus contain unflattering and embarrassing content portraying the disciples as scared and slow to believe, even exposing Thomas as a doubter. This gives reason to conclude that the authors were interested in recording the truth, regardless of how awkward these portrayals were for the early church.

Also, consider the somewhat embarrassing differences between the resurrection stories in the Gospels—for example, the number of angels at the tomb differ in the Gospel narratives. These differences don't represent contradictions or undermine our confidence in Scripture because they can be harmonized with little difficulty. But the fact that the authors didn't iron these out or smooth them over speaks to the fact that the writers didn't collude together to make sure their stories were exactly the same. Instead, they recorded what they themselves witnessed or what was reported to them by eyewitnesses.

Another example of the embarrassment criterion is the presence of women at the tomb. The Gospels tell us that women were the key eyewitnesses to the resurrection. In that culture, women were not even allowed to testify in a court of law because their testimony was considered untrustworthy.* Women were seen as second-class citizens in first-century Jewish culture. So, if you wanted to convince people in the ancient world that your leader was raised from the dead—and you are making up the story— you do not make women the eyewitnesses of that event. You make up a story wherein respected religious scholars were at the tomb to discover his resurrected body. And yet here, pushing against common sense, tradition, and culture, the testimony is given by women (John 20:1–2, 11–18). In fact, in all four Gospel narratives the first ones to arrive at the empty tomb are women. There would

---

* For instance, Josephus says: "Let not the testimony of women be admitted, on account of the levity and boldness of their sex" (*Antiquities* 4.8.15).

have been tremendous pressure to eliminate them from the story, but the writers do not. It is as if they are saying, "Take it or leave it. This is just what happened."

All of these criteria together provide good historical reasons to believe that the Gospel authors were recording history, not making up a story or engaging in an elaborate hoax. But there is even more compelling data to consider when investigating whether Jesus really rose from the dead.

THE RISE OF THE CHURCH

The last, and perhaps the most convincing, piece of evidence for the resurrection of Jesus is the rise of the early church—the surprising fact that out of nowhere, and almost overnight, a small band of Jews went from a conservative, scared, and irrelevant group to excited revolutionaries. What else but the resurrection would cause them to start worshiping a man

> Any person who is skeptical about the resurrection of Jesus needs to come up with an adequate explanation for why the disciples would create such an elaborate hoax and then be willing to die for it.

(which would have been blasphemous), claiming he rose from death, and then suffer torture and death themselves because of it?

Any person who is skeptical about the resurrection of Jesus needs to come up with an adequate explanation for why the disciples would create such an elaborate hoax and then be willing to die for it. This action subverts everything we know about human nature. If there was no resurrection, we would have to believe that these followers, and their families, unanimously held to something they knew was not true and suffered torture, pain, and death because of it.

It might be objected that lots of people die for lies they think are true. But who dies for a lie *they know isn't true*—for something they made up? Jesus' own brother James was tortured and killed, all of which could have been stopped if he had recanted. But he never did. Either he died for something he was convinced was true to his core and was worth dying for, or he died for a lie he himself made up. I find the former far more convincing than the latter.

Most martyrs die for a set of beliefs they have been taught and become convinced of. In the disciples' case, they were not merely dying for a set of beliefs. They were dying for their testimony that they had personally seen the risen Jesus alive after he had been publicly crucified in Jerusalem. On the principle that liars make poor martyrs, they were almost surely telling the truth. But if they were telling the truth, then it means Jesus really was alive after he had been crucified and the whole story can't be a made-up hoax or a conspiracy.

J. Warner Wallace, an ex-homicide detective, points out that when you are looking for the real explanation for what happened in a situation like a murder (or its reverse) you must always resist conspiracy theories.[7] True conspiracies are actually quite rare, since they are extremely hard to pull off: you need to keep the lies straight, you need deep forms of communication, and often more than one or two people need to know the truth. Ideally, for a conspiracy to succeed, only two people should know about it—and once the deed is done, one needs to kill the other one.

According to Wallace, successful conspiracies share a few characteristics: a small number of conspirators, thorough and immediate communication, and little to no pressure applied on the people or the story. None of these was the case with Christianity: Jesus appeared to over five hundred people after his resurrection who were going around claiming that he was alive (1 Corinthians 15:6); there was no way to quickly communicate among those people, as these were the days before email and text; and the highest level of pressure was applied, namely, torture and death of the disciples and their loved ones. Based on the best historical evidence we have, here is what seemingly happened to the original disciples of Jesus:

- Andrew was crucified in Patras, Greece.

- Bartholomew (aka Nathaniel) was flayed to death with a whip in Armenia.

- John died in exile on the island of Patmos.

- James the Greater (brother of John) was beheaded in Jerusalem.

- Luke was hanged in Greece.

- Mark was dragged by a horse to death in Alexandria, Egypt.

- Matthew was killed by sword in Ethiopia.

- Matthias was stoned and then beheaded in Jerusalem.

- Peter was crucified upside down in Rome.

- Philip was crucified in Phrygia.

- Thomas was stabbed to death with a spear in India.[8]

Not only does all of this evidence counter the idea that the resurrection was a hoax, it highlights again the unlikely rise of the early church. Overnight, a group of poor peasants starts to claim something completely against their worldview, and one of the fastest and most influential movements in the history of the world is born. Under persecution from both the Jews and the Roman Empire, Christianity grew to over 33 million people in just 350 years; by AD 400, 56 percent of the population of the Roman Empire were Christians.[9] Why did it grow so quickly? Why were men and women, even close family and friends, so willing to die for Christianity?

> They weren't dying for a set of metaphorical religious teachings, or for principles of life taught them by a dead sage, but for a claim about what had happened to Jesus *after* he died.

Jesus' followers died *because* they claimed that they had seen Jesus rise from the dead. They were persecuted and tortured and told to recant this claim, but they never did. They weren't dying for a set of metaphorical religious teachings, or for principles of life taught to them by a dead sage, but for a claim about what had happened to Jesus *after* he died. If Jesus really died for sins and rose again, then everything he taught was vindicated as true. His teachings were an anchor of hope, including his perspective on eternal life wherein he explained, "The one who believes in me will live, even though they die; and whoever lives by believing in me will never die" (John 11:25–26). His followers took this to heart. They weren't deterred by death. They were willing to be sawn in half, stretched apart, thrown to the lions in gladiatorial arenas, or stoned to death in the street. They never recanted their testimony, and that conviction, courage, and hope caused the gospel to spread very quickly in the ancient world.[10] The scholar R. H. Fuller has pointed out that "even the most skeptical critic must posit some mysterious X that got the Christian movement going. But what was that X?"[11] The New Testament claims it was the resurrection.

THE NATURALISTIC OBJECTION

The historical evidence strongly indicates that Jesus actually rose from the dead. Some people, however, tend to resist this conclusion for philosophical or scientific reasons. Some hold to a naturalistic worldview, which says there is by definition no supernatural explanation for anything that happens, thereby rejecting the explanation of the resurrection even in the face of historical evidence. The fundamental issue for a naturalist is that, according to everything we know about nature from our experience, it is implausible that a corpse would return to life because "the causal powers of nature are insufficient" to do that.[12] This was my issue as a skeptic. But I came to see that this logic is actually irrelevant to assessing the plausibility of the resurrection, or any other miracle, because the proposition of Christianity isn't that nature by itself reversed or did something unique that had never been done before and has never been done since. Instead, Christianity taught that *God* raised Jesus from the dead. God "raised Christ from the dead and seated him at his right hand in the heavenly realms," the apostle Paul says in his letter to the Ephesians (1:20). The apostle Peter in his sermon on the day of Pentecost tells the crowd, "But God raised him from the dead, freeing him from the agony of death" (Acts 2:24).

Christians don't believe the resurrection was a natural event. The resurrection was a *super*natural act of a God who transcends nature itself. If there is good evidence to believe that God exists, which other contributors to this book have outlined, then miracles are possible.[13] And the best explanation for the data surrounding the birth of Christianity is that God raised Jesus from the dead. The bottom line may be that the naturalist position is nothing more than a philosophical prejudice that impedes a fair assessment of the available evidence that undergirds the Christian faith.

From a naturalistic perspective, the resurrection is unbelievable because it goes against the laws of nature. But if God exists, there is no reason to believe he can't feed new and surprising events into the course of nature. In fact, from a theological perspective, God in these miraculous acts is doing something that is not contrary to nature or in violation of it. Instead, God's signs and wonders are restorative. According to the Bible, death, decay, entropy, and destruction, at least as they apply to people, are the true violations of nature as God intended, and miracles are the early glimpses of restoration. In that way, the words of Jürgen Moltmann about Jesus' healings can be applied to God's miracles in general: they "are not supernatural miracles in a natural world. They are the only

truly 'natural' thing in a world
that is unnatural, demonized
and wounded."[14] God's miraculous intervention brings creation
back to what it was intended to

> God's miraculous
> intervention brings
> creation back to what
> it was intended to be
> before sin and death
> entered the world.

be before sin and death entered the world through the
sin of people. The resurrection is both a glance back to
the garden before evil and sin existed as well as a pointer
toward the promised new creation to come.[15]

CONCLUSION:
WHAT DOES IT MEAN FOR US?

In a way, I have done this all backward. The resurrection
isn't just about what happened to Jesus, as important as
that was, but about who he is now, and thus, what we
should do about his identity as the resurrected Lord and
ascended King. Jesus may have been a poor Jewish peas-
ant two thousand years ago, but he isn't that now. No
longer is he a victim of death and torture, but a victori-
ous and risen King who holds the universe in his hand
(Revelation 1:12–16).

If the resurrection is true, it was the beginning of a
new creation. A new chapter opened in cosmic history,

and thus anyone who wants to benefit from this resurrection and enter a new kind of life themselves—not only in the future, but in the present as well—is now invited to participate in new life through Christ. The resurrection means that we, as human beings, don't need to keep flailing and floundering under the burden of religion. We don't need to keep setting aflame sacrifices so the gods will relent from their wrath or set out on a sacred pilgrimage so we can earn our way into divine favor. Jesus stumbled under the weight of a cross on his back. He underwent an excruciating death for us. Religion crushed him so it wouldn't have to crush us. The fire was kindled and directed toward him on the cross, and God's righteous judgment satisfied. Jesus took the ultimate pilgrimage for us, down from heaven to earth and back, so we wouldn't ever have to earn our way into God's favor through our own religious efforts.

Christianity says God came down the mountain to us. This is the scandal of the Easter message. Jesus rose from the dead, because first he died. And why did he die? Because we needed him to, whether we know it or not or asked for it or not. Jesus took on the sin of the world, and the resurrection says that sin was indeed paid for. Thus we can live in the freedom of a life without the debt of sin hanging over our heads and the power of sin clinging to our hearts. "Just as Christ was raised from the dead through the glory of the Father, we too may live a new life," Paul says in Romans 6:4. The resurrection was about Jesus, yes, and about the Father and how he was reconciling the world to himself, of course, but it was also about you and me. It was about us walking and living in a kind of newness that we cannot even imagine before we know it by experience. Temptations and identities that once ruled us and ruined us can burn away and no longer control our lives, our marriages, and our money. Lies we once told ourselves can dissipate in the light of new truths. Relationships once thought dead and gone can blossom again. Sickness can be overcome. Guilt can be banished and shame buried for good, left behind like grave clothes, for others seeking new life to find and ponder.

On and on I could go, but you get the picture: life, not death; light, not darkness; power, not burden. This is what the resurrection, and Christianity, says life is about: a story of lives being remade and a new way to be human opening up to all of us through the death and resurrection of Jesus.

Not only that, but death no longer has the final say. This is why we can wake up tomorrow and face the day, even when those we love may not. Such is the ultimate hope that Christianity offers.

10. The Search for the Meaning of Life

ANDY STEIGER

I n 2010, I founded an organization called Apologetics Canada. My wife and I began this ministry to help people think through life's big questions. From years of conversations, research, and working with young adults, it became clear to me that people were asking tough questions that churches were not taking seriously enough.

Sadly, I also learned that many young adults were leaving their Christian faith because they believed this lack of engagement was because there were no answers to their questions. Since starting Apologetics Canada, my desire has been to reintroduce others to Christianity's thoughtful answers to the important questions we're wrestling with, such as "What is the meaning of life?"

This particular question has special significance for me given my upbringing. As I reflected on Christianity's answer to this question, it not only made sense of my life, but also changed how I live it. The meaning of life is more than an intellectual question; it speaks to the very heart of human existence.

THE CAREER CASTE SYSTEM

I grew up in a poor and broken family. My parents separated when I was four years old, leaving my mother to raise four children on her own. She worked hard at a bank to care for us, doing everything in her power to give us a chance at life. In many ways, my mom sacrificed her dreams and desires for the sake of her children. Perhaps that's why I've never forgotten the way she would pull me aside while I was growing up and say, "Andy, I know you will do great things with your life."

I knew my mom meant those words to encourage me, but instead they became a burden. When you're a kid, doing great things is fairly easy, like graduating from diapers or learning to ride a bike. However, the older I got, the more complicated it became. I didn't want to disappoint my mom, but at the same time I had no idea how to accomplish "great things." I mean, what exactly qualifies?

We all have that sense deep within us for something more. We all want to make something of our lives, but we're not sure exactly how. Ultimately, these desires left me frustrated and anxious.

While I was in high school, I had very little self-esteem and almost no drive to do anything with my life. I had just given up. Life was quickly becoming meaningless. Eventually, this attitude led me to peers with a similar outlook. It didn't take long before we began to seek answers with alcohol and drugs. Over time, we felt a push toward harder alcohol and drugs in an attempt to achieve what the previous high could not. One day, as I was offered some harder drugs, I clearly saw that I had arrived at a crossroads; I needed to choose which direction my life would go. Saint Augustine (AD 354–430), a renowned Christian thinker, said that the human heart is restless.[1] That was exactly how I felt. I didn't know the answer I was seeking, but I knew where it couldn't be found. That day I gave up on alcohol and drugs.

However, what I was really doing was just swapping one high for another. Unsure of how to satisfy my restlessness without alcohol and drugs, I instead followed culture. Without really thinking about it, I began to occupy my restless energy with a life of accomplishment.

Western culture defines people by their accomplishments. After all, what are the first two questions we ask people when we meet them for the first time? "What's your name?" and "What do you do for a living?" The answers to those questions tell us everything we need to know to judge their success, and ultimately their worth, by Western standards. We may call it "climbing the corporate ladder," but it's really a career caste system; some careers are at the top and some are at the bottom, and nobody is confused about which is which. Dress your profession up with a technical name, but at the end of the day, who are we really fooling? If we're honest with ourselves, we are all guilty of placing others and ourselves in the career caste system.

> Without really thinking about it, I began to occupy my restless energy with a life of accomplishment.

When I graduated from high school, I found myself overwhelmed by all of the different types of accomplishments I could pursue. I decided to start by tackling college. Considering that no one in my family had ever earned a degree, this seemed like a good place to begin an assault on "great things." It wasn't long until I had a good list of achievements under my belt: I graduated from college, hiked to Mount Everest, got married, traveled the world, bought a house, had kids, completed a master's degree, and founded an organization.

For a while, accomplishment climbing worked; I found that reaching my goals was exhilarating! Standing on top of my accomplishments provided me a brief high, a flash of relief, and for a moment my restless heart was calmed. I felt on top of the world, with the view of my accomplishments stretched out beneath me. In those moments, I wanted to yell out: "This is it! I've made it! This is what I live for!"

Yet it never lasted. Soon the moment would pass, my restlessness would come flooding back, and I would descend another of life's peaks frustrated.

VALLEY FLOOR

What is true of mountain ranges is also true of life: you can't have mountains unless you have valleys.

Accomplishment climbing, or pleasure seeking through drugs, alcohol, and sex, ensures that we will have low times of restlessness and despair. It's in these valleys where we begin to fix our attention on the next summit, setting our sights continually higher in hopes that the next high will achieve what the previous couldn't. So begins a never-ending cycle, a progression of peaks and valleys, with the peaks growing ever higher and the valleys sinking ever deeper. It shouldn't surprise us when so many people struggle with a midlife crisis or hit rock bottom. With each new peak comes an equally difficult valley, until eventually the valley becomes so deep you just can't get out of it anymore. Before we set our sights too high and descend too low, we can learn from those who have climbed higher than us.

> Before we set our sights too high and descend too low, we can learn from those who have climbed higher than us.

One of my favorite comedians is Jim Carrey. He's funny, wealthy, and famous. Yet in a 2014 commencement speech, he said, "I've often said that I wished people could realize all their dreams of wealth and fame, so they could see that it's not where you'll find your sense of completion."[2]

This is exactly what King Solomon experienced. Solomon was the king of Israel from around 970–931 BC and was renowned for having everything. He was intelligent, wealthy, and powerful, yet none of that satisfied him. In the book of Ecclesiastes, he wrote:

> I said to myself, "Come on, let's try pleasure. Let's look for the 'good things' in life." But I found that this, too, was meaningless. So I said, "Laughter is silly. What good does it do to seek pleasure?" After much thought, I decided to cheer myself with wine. And while still seeking wisdom, I clutched at foolishness. In this way, I tried to experience the only happiness most people find during their brief life in this world. ... I even found great pleasure in hard work, a reward for all my labors. But as I looked at everything I had worked so hard to accomplish, it was all so meaningless—like chasing the wind. There was nothing really worthwhile anywhere. (Ecclesiastes 2:1–11 NLT)

In today's culture, we don't usually envy kings like Solomon. Instead, we envy people like Tom Brady. He is arguably the greatest quarterback of all time; he's wealthy, athletic, and has a supermodel for a wife. Yet in a 2005 TV interview he said, "Why do I have three Super Bowl rings and still think there's something greater out there for me? I mean, maybe a lot of people would say, 'Hey man, this is what it is.' I reached my goal, my dream, my life. Me, I think, 'God, it's got to be more than this.'" The interviewer quickly asked, "What's the answer?" Tom responded, "I wish I knew. I wish I knew."[3]

At some level, don't statements like these shock us? It's difficult to believe that the things we think would surely satisfy us didn't satisfy those who accomplished them!

> That's the problem with wealth, success, and greatness: there's always more wealth to acquire, more to succeed at, and there will always be someone greater than you.

That's because there truly is no top, no ultimate peak that will satisfy. Instead, there are only varying levels of success, with all of us jostling for position. Even those who have climbed Everest experience this. Sure, it's the tallest mountain, but they still ask each other: "Which route did you take? What support did you have? Did you do it with oxygen tanks? How many times have you summited?"

It's not surprising that our accomplishments never satisfy. How can they? That's the problem with wealth, success, and greatness: there's always more wealth to acquire, more to succeed at, and there will always be someone greater than you.

The news is full of celebrities who testify to this through their addictions, obsessions, and depression. They're a constant reminder that it's never enough. Sex, drugs, and accomplishments will never satisfy you. What's the alternative? If your name and profession don't define you, what should?

This eventually led me to look outside of my accomplishments to satisfy my restless heart. I took a step back from culture and began a new journey to answer one of life's big questions: What is the meaning of life?

WHAT IS MEANING?

Things don't get their meaning merely from existing. Instead, meaning comes when someone with the power to do so, such as an author or creator, *gives* it.

For example, think of music. When a musician plays a note, which is just a mechanical wave of pressure that the human brain interprets as a specific sound, and strings it together with other notes in such a way as to invoke a certain emotion, then adds lyrics that convey the musician's heart, everyone recognizes that meaning has been created. What started as merely sound becomes music when it is infused with meaning. That's what artists, composers, and authors do; they endow the objects of their creation with information, significance, purpose, and worth. Only then can something be said to have meaning. The philosopher Thomas V. Morris says, "It follows from this that in any sense of the word 'meaning,' if anything in my life is to have meaning (or *a* meaning), it must be endowed with meaning. It must be *given* meaning. Meaning is never intrinsic; it is always derivative."[4] Meaning has to be *given* to something—it must come from an author.

But can't we just give our own lives meaning? That question draws attention to the two forms of meaning: subjective and objective. Subjective meaning is the personal significance we give to another person's work. This type of meaning changes from person to person. The love song I first danced to with my wife is full of meaning for me—but it's subjective meaning. On the other hand, objective meaning is the meaning we give to the things we create or control. Because it is based on the intent of the author, objective meaning will remain the same for everyone. For example, the composer of that same love song could tell me the reason he wrote it; that would be the objective meaning.

Sometimes we can know something has meaning, but it can be difficult to tell what that meaning is. Prior to 1822, the markings that cover the ancient structures and artifacts of Egypt were a complete mystery. It was obvious that the ancient Egyptians had given the markings meaning, and that together they made up a language, but the meaning had been lost to time. Scholars made a variety of guesses, but no amount of study could decipher them. The ancient language of the Egyptians was dead because the meaning had been lost.

> Because it is based on the intent of the author, objective meaning will remain the same for everyone.

This began to change in 1799, when a rock was discovered near Alexandria, Egypt, in the town of Rosetta (Rashid). On it was written the same message in three scripts: Egyptian hieroglyphs, Demotic, and ancient Greek. It took over twenty years, but using the meaning from Greek and other languages, scholars were able to rediscover the meaning of Egyptian hieroglyphs. The once-dead language suddenly came alive again. If you have ever studied a foreign language, computer code, or texting acronyms, you know what it's like for strange markings, symbols, and letter combinations to come alive once their meaning is explained to you. This is exactly what the Rosetta Stone accomplished.

Before 1822, a person could have studied Egyptian hieroglyphs and ascribed whatever meaning they wanted to the symbols. But that meaning would not have been the objective meaning. That meaning would have been subjective. In order to actually read the language, we needed to know the objective meaning, the intended meaning given it by its authors, in this case the ancient Egyptians.

What if the same is true of life? Could human life be like a dead language containing a treasure of knowledge, significance, worth, and purpose, just waiting to be rediscovered? Is this why we are restless? We keep trying to read a dead language by giving it subjective meaning, but nothing makes sense. We sense that our lives have an objective meaning, but we don't know how to access it.

THE BARE NECESSITIES

One day when I came home from work, I found one of my son's "hieroglyphic" stick figure drawings taped to his bedroom door. It contained four figures—two large and two small. The two large stick figures were circled with a line through them. "That doesn't look good," I thought to myself. Now, I could have taken an educated guess at what the picture meant, but I might have been wrong. Likewise, I could have given it personal significance, but I would still be no closer to understanding its intended meaning. To discover the intended meaning of anything, you need to somehow access the author who created it. In this case, it was easy: I asked

To discover the intended meaning of anything, you need to somehow access the author that created it.

my son. After a few questions, I learned that the drawing meant Mom and Dad were not allowed to come into his room during wrestling matches with his younger brother. In other words, he didn't want us to stop him from beating up his younger brother. Well, that wasn't going to happen!

Just as objective meaning was necessary in order to understand hieroglyphs or my son's drawing, objective meaning is necessary in order to decipher the meaning of life. Subjective meaning is just not capable of answering questions like "Why am I here?" and "What meaning was

I created for?" Answering those foundational questions requires objective meaning, found only in the creator of life—God.

Now, I'm not saying that you need to believe in God in order to live a subjectively meaningful life. I believe that people can give their lives personal meaning and significance without appealing to God. In fact, we do it all the time. I have a love for hiking, and this passion does contribute to my life.

But what I'm talking about is much more basic. I want to know why I exist. The truth is, we did not bring ourselves into existence. Thus, it is beyond our control to give the whole of human life, or our own life in particular, objective meaning. Morris explains this well when he says:

So what exactly is outside the scope of our control? Well, to put it bluntly, nothing more than birth, life, suffering, and death. And if all this is outside our control, we do not have the requisite control to see to it that our lives are completely meaningful, through and through, from first to last. We can create islands of meaning in this sea of existence we've been given, but ... it seems that anything we build we will build with materials that have been given to us.[5]

This is why a search for the meaning of life inevitably leads to questions about the origins of life and the existence of God.

JESUS' ANSWER TO THE MEANING OF LIFE

As I mentioned above, in order for something to have objective meaning, it needs to have been given it by the person who authored or created it. Since people did not bring themselves into existence, we can't be our own author. Instead, we need someone who created the universe and human life in particular. We need someone like God. Simply put: if God exists, life has objective meaning, and if God does not exist, our lives have only the subjective meaning we give them, which is no better than accomplishment climbing or pleasure seeking. In the end, subjective meaning is unable to satisfy our restless desire for something deeper. I began to wonder, What if subjective meaning is unable to satisfy because there is a reason humanity exists? I wanted to discover that objective meaning that makes sense of my life, and see if it does satisfy.

For this reason, my journey for meaning began with a search for God, which led me to Jesus, who not only claimed to be the Author of life but gave an answer to the meaning of life.[6] Jesus' teaching on the meaning of life can be clearly seen in a dialogue found in the Bible in Mark 12. There we are told that those listening to Jesus were impressed by his answers to tough questions, so they decided to press him. An expert in Jewish law asked Jesus: "Of all the commandments, which is the most important?" This is the ancient Jewish equivalent of asking, "What's the meaning or purpose of life? What's the most important thing to know?"

> if God exists, life has objective meaning, and if God does not exist, our lives have only the subjective meaning we give them, which is no better than accomplishment climbing or pleasure seeking.

"The most important one," answered Jesus, "is this: Hear, O Israel, the Lord our God, the Lord is one." In other words, Jesus reminded them that life has only one Author—God. He then said these famous words: "Love the Lord your God with all your heart and with all your soul and with all your mind and with all your strength. The second is this: Love your neighbor as yourself. There is no commandment greater than these" (Mark 12:30–31).

The meaning of life, defined by Jesus, is simple: love God. The message of the Bible from beginning to end repeats this same message: God loves humankind and created us for relationship. Each one of us was created to know and be known, to love and be loved. In fact, those listening would instantly have recognized that Jesus is quoting the Shema, a prayer that occurs in Deuteronomy 6:4–9:

> The meaning of life, defined by Jesus, is simple: love God.

> Hear, O Israel: The LORD our God, the LORD is one. Love the LORD your God with all your heart and with all your soul and with all your strength. These commandments that I give you today are to be on your hearts. Impress them on your children. Talk about them when you sit at home and when you walk along the road, when you lie down and when you get up. Tie them as symbols on your hands and bind them on your foreheads. Write them on the doorframes of your houses and on your gates.

However, Jesus added something to the Shema, a summary of Leviticus 19 in which God explains to Moses how his people are to treat one another. He starts by saying, "Be holy because I, the LORD your God, am holy" (Leviticus 19:2). Then, God explains to Moses what holiness looks like in our relationships, summarizing it by saying, "Do not seek revenge or bear a grudge against a fellow Israelite, but love your neighbor as yourself. I am the LORD" (Leviticus 19:18 NLT). Jesus consistently taught that your love for God and his love for you will inspire you to become more like him—holy—and that this will lead you to show love for other people. In fact, Jesus taught that people will know you belong to him if you love one another (John 13:35). However, we need to get the order right. First and foremost, we were created to love God because God first loved us (1 John 4:19). It's from our relationship with God that we learn to love one another.

Jesus was a living demonstration of the lengths that God would go to so he could make his love known. The Bible explains that Jesus is the Author of life—God in the flesh. Instead of revealing himself as a far-off idea or cosmic guru, God willingly left heaven and came to earth as a baby to make himself known in a way that we could understand—as a human being. It's hard to express the scandal of that: the one who is greater than everything in existence came close enough for us to touch, near enough to be seen sweating, weeping, and bleeding.

The vast majority of the Bible is narrative; it's the story of God and his people. At the beginning, we were in a right and loving relationship with God, but then we rejected him and severed the relationship. God, however, did not give up on us. He sent his Son Jesus as a servant in order to bring us back into relationship with himself.

CONCLUSION: RELATIONALLY MADE

History is full of men and women who, in the search for meaning, were led to God. I was one of them. After Augustine claimed the human heart was restless, he went on to say to God, "You have made us for yourself, and our heart is restless until it rests in you."[7] The meaning of life is more than an intellectual question; it speaks to the very nature of what and who we are. We were made to live in relationship with God.

We don't need to go through the peaks and valleys of life alone; we were meant to experience all of life together in community with God and each other. That's where true meaning is found both now and in eternity—relationship.

Jesus' answer to the meaning of life changed my life because it changed my focus. I no longer look to people or my accomplishments to satisfy me—they can't. I am satisfied by living for God's glory rather than my own. This doesn't mean that the peaks and valleys of life are gone; in many ways my relationship with God has encouraged me to climb even higher. I just stopped trying to find my meaning in my accomplishments. We don't need to go through the peaks and valleys of life alone; we were meant to experience all of life together in community with God and each other. That's where true meaning is found both now and in eternity—relationship.

List of Contributors

Jason Ballard is the co-host of the Alpha Youth film series, which has been translated into dozens of languages and been seen by hundreds of thousands of young people around the world. Jason is a sought-after youth and young adult conference speaker. He has substantial experience answering the objections that young people have to the Christian faith and is well connected to many of the youth ministry organizations throughout North America and the world, including Hillsong's youth ministry.

Paul Chamberlain is the director of the Institute of Christian Apologetics at Trinity Western University and the author of five books, including *Why People Stop Believing* (2018). He has also written numerous articles on apologetics and ethical issues. Paul is a sought-after communicator and debater on topics related to Christian apologetics.

Mark Clark is the founder and pastor of Village Church, the fastest-growing church in Canada with over 5,000 weekly attendees (www.thisisvillagechurch.com). He is author of the book *The Problem of God* (2017). He has a master's in New Testament studies from Regent College and speaks throughout North America.

Kirk Durston has a PhD in biophysics. He is a lecturer, writer, and debater with Power to Change, a global ministry with huge impact on college campuses all over the world. Kirk has wide experience writing and speaking on issues of faith and science to students and laypeople.

Michael Horner has a master's degree in philosophy. As a lecturer with Power to Change, he has four decades of experience speaking, writing, blogging, and debating on university campuses around the world about the Christian faith. He has debated all manner of individuals and is featured in a number of well-publicized debates with atheists.

Jon Morrison is a sought-after communicator, debater, and spokesperson for the validity and truthfulness of the Christian worldview. Jon has written two bestselling books, *Clear Minds & Dirty Feet* (2013) and *Life Hacks* (2017). You can find Jon at www.jonmorrison.ca or somewhere in Abbotsford, BC, where he lives with his wife Hayley and their two girls, Abigail and Grace.

Chris Price served as the lead pastor at Calvary Baptist (Coquitlam, BC) for ten years before moving to pursue church planting in Vancouver. He has a master's in Christian studies and a BA in biblical studies, and he is the author of *Radical Hope: Resurrection Faith in a Hurting World* (2016). He is also a contributor to the UK-based Youth Alpha video teaching series and sometimes co-hosts a weekly podcast called Hidden City, which explores the hidden ideas that influence our lives today.

Barton Priebe is the lead pastor of Central Baptist Church, an urban community located in the downtown core of Victoria, Canada. He previously worked for four years as a resident director at Trinity Western University and served as the lead pastor at Dunbar Heights Baptist Church in Vancouver for thirteen years. He is currently working on a DMin at Northwest Baptist Seminary and is the author of *The Problem with Christianity: Six Unsettling Questions You've Asked* (2015).

Andy Steiger is the founder and director of Apologetics Canada, an organization dedicated to helping churches better understand and engage with today's culture. He created and hosted the award-winning video series The Human Project in partnership with Power to Change. In 2018 The Human Project debuted at film festivals around the globe and won a number of awards, including People's Choice and Best Short Film. Andy also created and hosted the Thinking Series and is the author of *Thinking? Answering Life's Five Biggest Questions* (2015). Andy speaks internationally at universities, conferences, churches, prisons, and coffee shops.

Notes

INTRODUCTION

1. Sean McDowell, *Apologetics for a New Generation* (Eugene, OR: Harvest House, 2009), 8.
2. C. S. Lewis, "Christian Apologetics," in *God in the Dock*, ed. Walter Hooper (HarperOne, 1994), 102.
3. Francis Spufford, *Unapologetic: Why, Despite Everything, Christianity Can Still Make Surprising Emotional Sense* (New York: HarperOne, 2013), 104.
4. *Apologetics for a New Generation*, 15.

CHAPTER 1

1. Gary Habermas, *Dealing with Doubt* (Chicago: Moody Press, 1990); available online at http://www.garyhabermas .com/books/dealing_with_doubt/dealing_with_doubt.htm.
2. C. S. Lewis, *Mere Christianity* (New York: HarperOne, 2001), 140.
3. Marilynne Robinson, *Gilead* (New York: Picador, 2004), 24.
4. For more on this program, check out *The Oxford Centre for Christian Apologetics* (www.theocca.org).
5. She tells the story of her season of doubt in *English Lessons: The Crooked Path of Growing toward Faith* (Colorado Springs: WaterBrook, 2017).
6. Richard Dawkins, "Lecture from 'The Nullifidian,'" The Richard Dawkins Foundation for Reason and Science,

http://old.richarddawkins.net/articles/89, December 9, 2013.

7. Mark Twain, *Following the Equator: A Journey Around the World* (Hartford, CT: American Publishing, 1898), 132.

8. See *My Utmost for His Highest,* December 15, "Approved Unto God" (Oswald Chambers Publications, 1963).

9. D. A. Carson, "Matthew," in *The Expositor's Bible Commentary: Matthew & Mark (Revised Edition)*, ed. Tremper Longman III and David E. Garland, vol. 9 (Grand Rapids, MI: Zondervan, 2010), 304–5.

10. Learn more about the Alpha program at alpha.org/about.

11. Matt Dillahunty, "Atheist Debates - Debate: Does science move us toward or away from God? With Jon Morrison," October 28, 2015, https://www.youtube.com/watch?v=7TQ44ZoUJgE.

CHAPTER 2

1. This quote appears at The Clergy Project's website, clergyproject.org.

2. This information was taken from the CA website: http://www.internetarchaeology.org/www.geocities.com/Athens/Academy/9104/index.html (accessed June 27, 2019).

3. The conversation with Ravi Zacharias to which I refer took place in the fall of 1999 in Atlanta, Georgia, at the RZIM head office.

4. The professor mentioned here is Dr. William Lane Craig, my apologetics professor at Trinity International University in 1980.

5. C. S. Lewis, *Mere Christianity* (San Francisco: HarperCollins, 1980), 161–62.

CHAPTER 3

1. Richard Dawkins, *The God Delusion* (Boston: Houghton Mifflin Company, 2008), 280.

2. Dawkins, *God Delusion*, 282.

3. Dawkins, *God Delusion*, 51 (emphasis mine).

4. Christopher Hitchens, *god is not Great: How Religion Poisons Everything* (Toronto: McClelland & Stewart, 2007), 101–2.

5. For a more detailed archeological description of these and other practices, see Clay Jones, "We Don't Hate Sin So We Don't Understand What Happened to the Canaanites," *Philosophia Christi* 11, no. 1 (2009): 53–72.

6. For a more detailed discussion of the material below, see Paul Copan, *Is God a Moral Monster? Making Sense of the Old Testament God* (Grand Rapids: Baker Books, 2011), chapters 15–17; Christopher J. H. Wright, *The God I Don't Understand* (Grand Rapids: Zondervan, 2008), chapters 4–5; and Joshua Ryan Butler, *The Skeletons in God's Closet: The Mercy of Hell, the Surprise of Judgment, the Hope of Holy War* (Nashville: Thomas Nelson, 2014), chapters 13–18.

7. Butler, *Skeletons in God's Closet*, 213–14.

8. Copan, *Is God a Moral Monster?*, 176.

9. Copan, *Is God a Moral Monster?*, 172.

10. Copan, *Is God a Moral Monster?*, 170–71.

11. "Driving out or dispossessing is different from wiping out or destroying. Expulsion is in view, not annihilation (e.g.,

'dispossess [*yarash*]' in Exod. 34:24; Num. 32:21; Deut. 4:38 NET). Just as Adam and Eve were 'driven out [*garash*]' of the garden (Gen. 3:24) or Cain into the wilderness (4:14) or David from Israel by Saul (1 Sam. 26:19), so the Israelites were to 'dispossess' the Canaanites." Copan, *Is God a Moral Monster?*, 181.

12. I once heard Dr. Timothy Keller make a similar argument in a sermon, and although I cannot locate when or where he said it, I give him credit for getting me to think along these lines.

13. Miroslav Volf, *Free of Charge: Giving and Forgiving in a Culture Stripped of Grace* (Grand Rapids: Zondervan, 2006), 138–39.

CHAPTER 4

1. J. K. Rowling, *Harry Potter and the Half-Blood Prince* (London: Bloomsbury, 2005), 177.

2. Gregory Boyd, "Love and Free Will," February 16, 2016, https://reknew.org/2016/02/love-and-free-will/.

3. J. B. S. Haldane, *Possible Worlds* (London: Chatto & Windus, 1927), 209.

4. Abdu Murray, *Saving Truth: Finding Meaning and Clarity in a Post-Truth World* (Grand Rapids: Zondervan, 2018), 103.

5. J. Warner Wallace, *God's Crime Scene: A Cold-Case Detective Examines the Evidence for a Divinely Created Universe* (Colorado Springs, CO: David C. Cook, 2015), 146.

6. C. S. Lewis, *Mere Christianity* (New York: HarperCollins, 1952), 47–48. Christian philosopher Alvin Plantinga states the free will defense in this manner: "A world containing

creatures who are significantly free (and freely perform more good than evil actions) is more valuable, all else being equal, than a world containing no free creatures at all. Now God can create free creatures, but He can't *cause* or *determine* them to do only what is right. For if He does so, then they aren't significantly free after all. ... To create creatures capable of moral good, therefore, He must create creatures capable of moral evil; and He can't give these creatures the freedom to perform evil and at the same time prevent them from doing so. As it turned out, sadly enough, some of the free creatures God created went wrong in the exercise of their freedom; this is the source of moral evil." Alvin Plantinga, *God, Freedom and Evil* (Grand Rapids: Eerdmans, 1974), 30.

7.   Dallas Willard, *The Allure of Gentleness: Defending the Faith in the Manner of Jesus* (New York: HarperCollins, 2015), 128.

8.   For a thorough examination of this matter, see Clay Jones, *Why Does God Allow Evil? Compelling Answers for Life's Toughest Questions* (Eugene, OR: Harvest House, 2017). In chapters 6–8 he even addresses questions like "Will we have free will in heaven?"

9.   John Hick, "An Irenaean Theodicy," in *Encountering Evil: Live Options in Theodicy*, ed. Stephen T. Davis (Louisville: John Knox, 1981), 47.

10.   In their book *Trauma & Transformation*, psychologists Richard G. Tedeschi and Lawrence G. Calhoun scrutinize the various psychological benefits of personal tragedy and testify that "apparently ordinary people achieve extraordinary wisdom through their struggles and circumstances that are initially aversive in the extreme." The authors

call this a "new and remarkable" discovery, but this is not a modern insight. Calhoun and Tedeschi, *Trauma & Transformation: Growing in the Aftermath of Suffering* (Thousand Oaks, CA: Sage, 1995), 2.

11. Willard, *The Allure of Gentleness*, 118.

12. Timothy Keller, *The Reason for God: Belief in an Age of Skepticism* (New York: Riverhead Books, 2008), 25.

13. John Stott, *The Cross of Christ* (Downers Grove, IL: InterVarsity Press, 1986), 335–36.

14. Lyrics from "God is Love" written by Timothy Rees in 1922.

15. Aleksandr Solzhenitsyn, *The Gulag Archipelago, 1918–1956: An Experiment in Literary Investigation* (New York: Collins Harvill, 1986), 312.

16. Marilyn McCord Adams, "Redemptive Suffering: A Christian Solution to the Problem of Evil," in L. Michael Peterson, ed., *The Problem of Evil: Selected Readings* (Notre Dame: University of Notre Dame Press, 1992), 179.

17. Quoted in Philip Yancey, *The Question That Never Goes Away* (Grand Rapids: Zondervan, 2013), 57–58.

18. For more help, see Nancy Guthrie, *What Grieving People Wish You Knew about What Really Helps (And What Really Hurts)* (Wheaton, IL: Crossway, 2016).

19. Quoted in Vaneetha Rendall Risner, *The Scars That Have Shaped Me: How God Meets Us in Suffering* (Minneapolis: Desiring God Publishing, 2016), 131.

20. Gregory Coles, *Single, Gay, Christian: A Personal Journey of Faith and Sexual Identity* (Downers Grove, IL: InterVarsity Press, 2017), 50.

CHAPTER 5

1. Arthur C. Clarke, *Childhood's End* (New York: Del Rey, 1953), 15.

2. Lisa Grossman, "Why physicists can't avoid a creation event," *New Scientist*, January 11, 2012, https://www.newscientist.com/article/mg21328474-400-why-physicists-cant-avoid-a-creation-event/.

3. "The Blue Cross," in *The Innocence of Father Brown* (New York: John Lane, 1911), 6.

4. Allison Terbosh, "Truth in science," http://berkeley-sciencereview.com/truth-in-science/.

5. Glenn Begley and Lee M. Ellis, "Raise Standards for Preclinical Cancer Research," *Nature* 483 (2012): 531–33.

6. Marcus Munafò, "Metascience: Reproducibility Blues," *Nature* 543 (2017): 619–20.

7. Michael Slezak, "Cosmic Inflation Is Dead, Long Live Cosmic Inflation!" *New Scientist*, September 25, 2014, https://www.newscientist.com/article/dn26272-cosmic-inflation-is-dead-long-live-cosmic-inflation/.

8. "Scientism," *Skeptic's Dictionary*, http://skepdic.com/scientism.html.

9. Jerry Fodor and Massimo Piattelli-Palmarini, "Survival of the Fittest Theory: Darwinism's Limits," *New Scientist*, February 3, 2010, https://www.newscientist.com/article/mg20527466-100-survival-of-the-fittest-theory-darwinisms-limits/.

10. "The origin of the very first species and the start of Darwinian evolution," Max-Planck-Gesellschaft,

November 23, 2015, https://www.mpg.de/9758765/evolution-first-species.

11. George Ellis and Joe Silk, "Scientific Method: Defending the Integrity of Physics," *Nature* 516 (2014): 321–23, https://www.nature.com/news/scientific-method-defend-the-integrity-of-physics-1.16535.

12. Philip Ball, "The Trouble with Scientists," *Nautilus*, May 14, 2015, http://nautil.us/issue/24/error/the-trouble-with-scientists.

13. George Ellis, "Cosmology: The Untestable Multiverse," *Nature* 469 (2011): 294–95.

14. Eugene Koonin, "The Cosmological Model of Eternal Inflation and the Transition from Chance to Biological Evolution in the History of Life," *Biology Direct* (June 2007), https://biologydirect.biomedcentral.com/articles/10.1186/1745-6150-2-15.

CHAPTER 6

1. C. S. Lewis, *Mere Christianity* (New York: HarperOne, 2001), 35.

2. A version of this story can be found in Jared C. Wilson, *Unparalleled: How Christianity's Uniqueness Makes It Compelling* (Grand Rapids: Baker Books, 2016), 231–32.

3. David Kinnaman and Gabe Lyons, *unChristian: What a New Generation Really Thinks about Christianity ... And Why It Matters* (Grand Rapids: Baker Books, 2007), 28.

4. A version of this story can be found in Timothy Keller, *The Prodigal Prophet: Jonah and the Mystery of God's Mercy* (New York: Viking, 2018), 183–84.

CHAPTER 7

1. Plato, *The Republic of Plato*, trans. A. D. Lindsay (New York: E.P. Dutton & Co, 1957).

2. "The Global Religious Landscape," Pew Research Religion and Public Life Project, December 18, 2012, http://www.pew-forum.org/2012/12/18/global-religious-landscape-exec/.

3. Justin L. Barrett, *Born Believers: The Science of Children's Religious Belief* (New York: Free Press, 2012), 3.

4. *Republic*, 257–64.

5. René Descartes, *Meditations on First Philosophy*, trans. Donald A. Cress (Indianapolis: Hackett, 1993), 13–16.

6. Nick Bostrom, "Are You Living in a Computer Simulation?," *Philosophical Quarterly* 53, no. 211 (2003): 243–55.

7. René Descartes, *Discourse on the Method of Rightly Conducting One's Reason and Seeking Truth in the Sciences*, trans. Jonathan Bennett, http://www.earlymoderntexts .com/pdfs/descartes1637.pdf

8. This estimate is according to the National Aeronautics and Space Administration (NASA). Their Cosmic Distance Scale feature, by Maggie Masetti, gives an excellent picture of just how big space is: https://imagine.gsfc.nasa.gov/ features/cosmic/ (accessed February 1, 2019).

9. The project was called the Hubble eXtreme Deep Field (XPF). To read more, visit https://www.nasa.gov/mission_ pages/hubble/science/xdf.html.

10. William Lane Craig and Quentin Smith, *Theism, Atheism and Big Bang Cosmology* (Oxford: Clarendon Press, 1993), 135.

11. "Special pleading" is a logical fallacy that happens "when someone uses a double standard or argues for an unjustified exception." See Nathaniel Bluedorn and Hans Bluedorn, *The Fallacy Detective: Thirty-Eight Lessons on How to Recognize Bad Reasoning* (Muscatine, IA: Christian Logic, 2009), 34.

12. Quoted in Lee Strobel, *The Case for a Creator: A Journalist Investigates Scientific Evidence That Points Toward God* (Grand Rapids: Zondervan, 2004), 101.

13. William Lane Craig, *Reasonable Faith: Christian Truth and Apologetics*, 3rd ed. (Wheaton, IL: Crossway, 2008), 154.

14. John Lennox, *God's Undertaker: Has Science Buried God?* 2nd ed. (Oxford: Lion, 2009), 66.

15. Antonina Vallentin, *The Drama of Albert Einstein* (New York: Doubleday, 1954), 24.

16. Due to problems of classification, sources listing the number of amino acids differ from one another. However, all sources that I consulted recognize between 20–23 amino acids.

17. Michael Denton, *Evolution: A Theory in Crisis* (Chevy Chase, MD: Adler & Adler, 1986), 334.

18. Bill Gates, *The Road Ahead* (London: Penguin, 1996), 228.

19. Stephen C. Meyer, *Signature in the Cell* (New York: HarperOne, 2009), 208–13.

20. Richard Dawkins, *The Blind Watchmaker: Why the Evidence of Evolution Reveals a Universe Without Design* (New York: W. W. Norton & Co., 1996), 1.

21. In my book *Thinking? Answering Life's Five Biggest Questions* (Abbotsford, BC: Apologetics Canada, 2015), I go into more detail regarding these arguments and their implications.

22.   C. S. Lewis, "Is Theology Poetry?," in *The Weight of Glory* (New York: HarperCollins, 2000), 140.

CHAPTER 8

1.   Luke A. Barnes, "The Fine-Tuning of Nature's Laws," *The New Atlantis* 47 (Fall 2015): 88–89, http://www.thenewatlantis.com/docLib/20160315_TNA47Barnes.pdf.

2.   Marcus Chown, "Anything Goes," *New Scientist* 158 (June 6, 1998): 28–29, cited at http://www2.asa3.org/archive/evolution/199806/0130.html.

3.   Barnes, "The Fine-Tuning of Nature's Laws," 90.

4.   Roger Penrose, "Time-Asymmetry and Quantum Gravity," in *Quantum Gravity 2*, ed. C. J. Isham, R. Penrose, and D. W. Sciama (Oxford: Clarendon, 1981), 249.

5.   William Lane Craig, *On Guard for Students: A Thinker's Guide to the Christian Faith* (Colorado Springs: David C. Cook, 2015), 93.

6.   Stephen W. Hawking and Leonard Mlodinow, *The Grand Design* (New York: Bantam, 2010), 143.

7.   Paul Davies, cited in William Lane Craig, *Reasonable Faith: Christian Truth and Apologetics* (Wheaton, IL: Crossway, 2008), 163.

8.   Leonard Susskind, "Leonard Susskind - Is the Universe Fine-Tuned for Life and Mind?," posted by Closer to Truth, January 8, 2013, https://www.youtube.com/watch?v=2cT4zZIHR3s. Comments at 6:15–6:41.

9.   Lewis and Barnes, *A Fortunate Universe: Life in a Finely Tuned Cosmos* (Cambridge: Cambridge University Press, 2016), 250.

10. Adapted from Lewis and Barnes, *A Fortunate Universe,* 250–53.

11. Lewis and Barnes, *A Fortunate Universe,* 321.

12. Craig, *On Guard for Students,* 101.

13. Barnes, "Fine-Tuning of Nature's Laws," 94.

14. John Horgan, "Physicist George Ellis Knocks Physicists for Knocking Philosophy, Falsification, Free Will," *Scientific American,* July 22, 2014, https://blogs.scientificamerican.com/cross-check/physicist-george-ellis-knocks-physicists-for-knocking-philosophy-falsification-free-will/.

15. Craig, *On Guard for Students,* 103.

16. For example, Craig, *On Guard for Students,* 98. Lewis and Barnes agree: "The conditional statement '*If* physical observers *then* an observer-permitting universe' does not answer the question: 'Why observers?'" Lewis and Barnes, *A Fortunate Universe,* 275.

17. See John Leslie, "How to Draw Conclusions from a Fine-Tuned Cosmos," in Robert Russell et al., eds., *Physics, Philosophy and Theology: A Common Quest for Understanding* (Vatican City: Vatican Observatory Press, 1988), 304; and John Leslie, "Anthropic Principle, World Ensemble, Design," *American Philosophical Quarterly* 19 (1982): 150.

18. Quoted in the transcript of William Lane Craig, "Fine Tuning Argument," Reasonable Faith, https://www.apologeet.nl/wp-content/uploads/documents/Transcript_Fine_Tuning_Argument.pdf.

19. Tim Barnett, "If the Universe Is Fine-Tuned, Why Is It Mostly Inhospitable for Life?" *Stand to Reason,* March 2,

2017, https://www.str.org/blog/if-universe-fine-tuned-why
-it-mostly-inhospitable-life.

20. Barnett, "Universe Is Fine-Tuned"; Lewis and Barnes, *A Fortunate Universe*, 247.

21. Lewis and Barnes, *A Fortunate Universe*, 250.

22. Paul Davies, *The Cosmic Blueprint: New Discoveries in Nature's Creative Ability to Order the Universe* (New York: Simon & Schuster, 1988), 203.

23. Alvin Plantinga, "The Dawkins Confusion: Naturalism 'ad absurdum,'" *Books and Culture* (March/April 2007): 4.

CHAPTER 9

1. Pindar, *Pythian Odes*, 3:1–60.

2. N. T. Wright, *The Resurrection of the Son of God* (Minneapolis: Fortress Press, 2003), 49.

3. Wright, *Resurrection*, 35.

4. Wright, *Resurrection*, 692.

5. See Sura 4:157 of the Qur'an.

6. See Edwin Yamauchi, "Jesus Outside the New Testament: What Is the Evidence?" in *Jesus Under Fire*, ed. M. J. Wilkins and J. P. Moreland (Grand Rapids: Zondervan, 1995), 212.

7. J. Warner Wallace, *Cold-Case Christianity: A Homicide Detective Investigates the Claims of the Gospels* (Colorado Springs, CO: David C. Cook, 2013), 109–12.

8. Wallace, *Cold-Case Christianity*, 115.

9. Rodney Stark, *The Rise of Christianity: A Sociologist Reconsiders History* (San Francisco: HarperSanFrancisco, 1996), 7.

10. Wright, *Resurrection*, chs. 18–19.

11. Quoted in William Lane Craig, "Jesus' Resurrection," Reasonable Faith, https://www.reasonablefaith. org/writings/scholarly-writings/historical-jesus/ jesus-resurrection/.

12. William Lane Craig, "Did Jesus Rise from the Dead?," *Jesus Under Fire*, 146.

13. See especially chapter 5, "Are Faith and Science in Conflict?"

14. Jürgen Moltmann, *The Way of Jesus Christ: Christology in Messianic Dimensions*, trans. Margaret Kohl (Minneapolis, MN: Fortress Press, 1993), 99.

15. Philip Yancey, *The Jesus I Never Knew* (Grand Rapids: Zondervan, 1995), 183.

CHAPTER 10

1. Saint Augustine, *The Confessions of Saint Augustine*, trans. John K. Ryan (New York: Doubleday, 1960), 43.

2. Jim Carrey, "Commencement Speech at Maharishi University of Management Graduation," May 24, 2014, https:// www. mum.edu/whats-happening/graduation-2014/ full-jim-carrey-address-video-and-transcript.

3. Tom Brady, "Tom Brady: The Winner," interview by Steve Kroft, *CBS: 60 Minutes,* November 6, 2005, http://www. cbsnews.com/news/tom-brady-the-winner/3/ (accessed February 11, 2019).

4. Thomas V. Morris, *Making Sense of It All: Pascal and the Meaning of Life* (Grand Rapids: Eerdmans, 1992), 56–57.

5. Morris, *Making Sense,* 61.

6. If you would like to read more about how I came to the conclusion that God exists and Jesus is who he claimed to

be, I encourage you to read my book *Thinking? Answering Life's Five Biggest Questions* (Abbotsford, BC: Apologetics Canada, 2015).

7.   Augustine, *Confessions*, 43.